PENGUIN BOOKS
THE CHILDREN OF THEATRE STREET

Earle Mack is executive vice-president of The Mack Company, a family enterprise established in 1896, specializing in property development. A 1975 tour of the Vaganova Choreographic Institute inspired Mack, a rabid devotee of classical dance, to think seriously about recording the inner workings of this legendary academy. His vision was realized the next year, when he became the first Western filmmaker to be allowed into the school, to film *The Children of Theatre Street*. In 1977 the documentary that he produced and co-directed was released in the United States and previewed abroad, to tremendous critical acclaim. Initially his passion for ballet grew out of his love for the beauty of thoroughbred racehorses, which he has owned and bred for the last fifteen years. "A dancer and a racehorse, when perfectly fit, are the ultimate in athleticism," he contends.

Patricia Barnes's interviews, articles, and ballet reviews have appeared in the London *Times*, *Dance News* magazine, and the British publication *Dance and Dancers*, for which she has been the New York correspondent since 1968. She has written brief biographies of Mikhail Baryshnikov and Maris Liepa for Dance Horizons and for several years worked on television dramas for A.T.V. (London). Mrs. Barnes is on the board of directors of the International League for Human Rights, and between the years 1972 and 1974 she worked actively to assist Valery and Galina Panov in their emigration from the U.S.S.R. Together with her husband, Clive, and their two teenage children, she has made New York City her home since 1965.

The Children of Theatre Street

·INTRODUCTION BY·

Earle Mack

·TEXT BY·

PATRICIA BARNES

Penguin Books

Penguin Books Ltd, Harmondsworth,
Middlesex, England
Penguin Books, 625 Madison Avenue,
New York, New York 10022, U.S.A.
Penguin Books Australia Ltd, Ringwood,
Victoria, Australia
Penguin Books Canada Limited, 2801 John Street,
Markham, Ontario, Canada L3R 1B4
Penguin Books (N.Z.) Ltd, 182–190 Wairau Road,
Auckland 10, New Zealand

First published in the United States of America in simultaneous hardcover
and paperback editions by The Viking Press and Penguin Books 1978

Text copyright © Patricia Barnes, 1978
Introduction and illustrations copyright © Earle Mack, 1978
All rights reserved

Library of Congress Cataloging in Publication Data
Barnes, Patricia.
    The children of Theatre Street.
    Bibliography: p. 142.
    Includes index.
    1. Leningrad. Gosudarstvennoe khoreograficheskoe
uchilishche. I. Title.
GV1788.6.L46B37   792.8′07′104745   78-13492
ISBN 0 14 00.5019 1

Printed in the United States of America by
The Murray Printing Company, Westford, Massachusetts
Set in Bodoni Book

Designed by Gael Towey Dillon

The rights to the film *The Children of Theatre Street* are reserved.
The film is available for distribution through
the Mack-Vaganova Production Co., 415 East 52nd Street,
New York, New York 10022,
(212) 755-2518.

Contents

Introduction by Earle Mack
6

1. A School of Dancing is Founded
11

2. The Children of Theatre Street Today
47

Acknowledgments
140

Photo Credits
141

Bibliography
142

Index
143

Introduction

An opportunity came out of the blue late one evening in April 1976.

That evening, Robert Dornhelm, a young Austrian television director, telephoned from Vienna. He had just returned from Leningrad, where he had been told by Soviet authorities that I had been granted permission to film at will inside the world-famous Vaganova Choreographic Institute, better known as the Kirov Ballet School.

For as long as I can remember, I have been patiently devoted to the ballet, not as a participant, but as that most rabid of devotees, the obsessive spectator. Appreciation, Wordsworth said, is next to excellence. But, for me, appreciation was not enough. I wanted somehow to participate.

I had pretty much given up on my request made while on tour of the Soviet Union the preceding winter. The tour was conducted by Oleg Briansky, the former dancer and authority on Russian ballet. On these annual tours, a dozen or so balletomanes are permitted to see the inner workings of this legendary academy, which has produced some of the world's greatest dancers. I believed then as I do now that what goes on behind those closed doors should be recorded and offered to those students, dancers, teachers, and balletomanes who do not have the means to see the Kirov as I and a handful of others have seen it.

Knowing enough about the Soviet bureaucracy to realize that my request had very little chance of being approved, I recklessly demanded virtual carte blanche. So much the greater was my surprise when the Russians actually granted it! I was to become the first Western filmmaker allowed into the Kirov to film "The Children of Theatre Street."

One of the reasons I had asked for so much was that I wasn't really sure I wanted it. I am, after all, a businessman, not a filmmaker. But I am an incurable balletomane. Initially, my love of ballet had grown out of my love for the beauty of racehorses in motion. (If this seems farfetched, read Edwin Denby's description of the girls of the New York City Ballet dancing Balanchine's *Caracole*, with their "spiky hooflike steps." He compares them to Lipizzaner horses. And, of course, a caracole is the horse's equivalent of a demi-tour.) A dancer's and a racehorse's conditioning and development are similar; for example, the extensions, the muscle toning, the building of stamina, and the importance of proper placement for a dancer are the same important ingredients that are necessary to develop a perfectly conditioned horse. The derivative injuries also are similar because of the intense strain put on the ankles, tendons, and knees of both dancers and horses. All in all, a dancer and a racehorse, when perfectly fit, are the ultimate in athleticism.

It was not without serious consideration that I decided to take the plunge and go ahead with the project. The schedule the Soviets outlined was incredibly tight. They wanted filming to begin in mid-May, which gave us just about a month to prepare. But this also gave us the opportunity to film the entire graduation performance at the Kirov Theatre, which to the best of my knowledge had never been filmed before.

My first order of business was to engage the artists and technicians who could realize my intentions, for movies are made of film, not just ideas. And, much as I would have liked to, I could not simply drop everything and run off to Russia to make a film. An unforeseen matter would unfortunately keep me in New York during much of the actual filming, although the constant telephone contact I maintained with the crew could almost have financed another film.

The young man who had brought me such glad tidings, Robert Dornhelm, had done many documentary reportages for Austrian television, including one on the school itself, and I decided to hire him as technical director (he was later to become co-director). Oleg Briansky was engaged as artistic director, to advise on technical matters relating to dance and to supervise the filming of the dance sequences. Jean Dalrymple, the renowned New York theatrical producer, publicist, and writer, joined us as associate producer. Karl Kofler, with whom Robert had worked previously, became director of photography.

I didn't have to consult my friends in Hollywood to know that documentary films, no matter how important or well made, rarely make money. Being an astute businessman, I know a poor investment when I see one and would not entice friends into supporting it. But this was something I had to do, and I proceeded with the optimistic rationalization that I might eventually break even.

The crew took off for the Soviet Union. The first stop was at the Novosti Press Agency in Moscow, which supplied assistant cameramen, interpreters, and administrative assistants. Then on to Leningrad, where filming began on May 15, 1976.

During the filming we had the complete cooperation of administrators, teachers, and students. Our hardworking Russian colleagues on the crew knew not of coffee breaks, unions, or overtime, and proved to be both competent and pleasant.

The crew filmed classes, rehearsals, and the entire graduation performance in the Kirov Theatre, as well as more informal moments in the hallways, dining hall, and students' rooms. We got some rare glimpses into contemporary Soviet life. Almost all the action was spontaneous.

Filming ended on June 5. Happily, I had been able to join the crew during the final week of shooting.

One of the most disconcerting aspects of filming in Leningrad was the impossibility of getting the film processed daily to look at the "rushes." In other words, the entire film was shot with our fingers crossed and with silent prayers that the cameras were working, the film was not defective, and the lighting was proper. The film was processed in London and sent on to Vienna, where Robert, Jean, and Tina Frese, our editor, made the first rough cut.

It was with a tremendous sense of anticipation and no small amount of anxiety that I made the trip to Vienna to view the footage for the first time. My anxiety was soon alleviated. The quality of the camerawork, the lighting, and the color were excellent.

But most of all I was impressed by the children themselves. I was struck by their discipline and dedication, their beauty and grace. The idea that had begun to occur to me on the set in Leningrad during the days I had spent with the crew now made more sense to me than ever, and I saw the film taking a new direction.

Rather than a purely "educational" product that would be of value to dancers, dance teachers, and dance students—in a word, to those who had already been "initiated" into the world of ballet—I saw the film as a means of creating a greater acceptance for dance in America among general audiences. I envisioned it as a film that could entertain as well as instruct. And the best way to do this was to concentrate on the children—specifically, on eleven-year-old Angelina Armeiskaya; her godmother, Lena Voronzova, who was graduating that year and joining the Kirov company; and Angelina's boyfriend, Alec Timoushin.

This required that we go back to Leningrad and shoot additional footage of the children. I went with Robert directly to Moscow and spoke to Novosti about obtaining the necessary permissions to reshoot; these were granted. But on the last day of our stay we heard rumblings that made us apprehensive about the outcome of the reshooting. It seemed that the Novosti film and television department was in danger of being dissolved. We were assured that our permissions would hold in any case, and thus journeyed to Leningrad to inform the school when to expect us back.

In New York the film was reedited under my constant supervision in anticipation of the new footage. I worked at my office by day, and by night, weekends, and early mornings at editing. A story theme was created and holes were left that would be filled by the new material. At this time a new member joined our team. Ted Landreth, a former television news executive who had been advising me for some time, was engaged as consultant to the producer. His experience in production and distribution proved to be invaluable when unforeseen complications arose.

We knew we had to work fast because of the rumor about Novosti. My fears were reinforced when all of us, in varying degrees, experienced difficulties and delays in obtaining visas, which heretofore had been forthcoming routinely. I realized then that we were taking a gamble and that the entire crew might be turned away at Moscow airport. But it was the only way the film could be finished. The execution of the whole project was touch-and-go from its inception, and it would have been inconsistent with the spirit of the film's existence if we had not taken the final plunge.

Upon our arival in Moscow, the State Committee for Television and Radio Broadcasting informed us that Novosti had been officially dissolved, and that our contract with them had become invalid. What to do? We couldn't just turn around and go home. Instead we rushed off to Leningrad at midnight and filmed in three and a half days what we had originally planned to film in seven. The filming itself was a tremendous success. We got some wonderful shots, and we were certain that we now had enough material to produce the film I envisioned. No small part of our success was due to the dedication of the former Novosti crew members, without whom the film could not have been completed.

The final editing took place in New York. At this time I engaged Beth Gutcheon to write the narration; then, knowing her love for the ballet, by prior suggestion of Oleg Briansky, I asked Princess Grace of Monaco if she would be interested in narrating the film. After seeing the final cut and reading the narration, she agreed to make a rare venture back into the film world in *The Children of Theatre Street*.

Meanwhile, I contacted the Soviet Ministry of Culture to confirm our plans to premiere the film in Moscow, with a reception to follow at the American Ambassador's residence. They were satisfied with the film, but informed us that unless we deleted from the script the names of the three defectors from the Kirov, Rudolf Nureyev, Natalia Makarova, and Mikhail Baryshnikov, there would be no Moscow premiere and no subsequent Soviet cooperation.

We protested not only that would this be contrary to our principles, but these names were household words in America and that it would be ludicrous to make a film about the Kirov School and not mention them. We had always assumed that while it was implicit in our agreement that we would not glorify the defectors, we certainly would mention them. The Soviets insisted on the deletions. We refused. The premiere was called off. They wanted no mention of any Soviet participation in the credits. They refused payment. We were naturally disappointed, but in good conscience we had no choice.

Instead of having its premiere in Moscow, *The Children of Theatre Street* had its first showing in New York City, as a gala to benefit the school that is the closest we have to a dance academy comparable to the Kirov in the United States, the School of American Ballet, which was founded by one of the Kirov's most illustrious graduates, George Balanchine.

Some months later the official opening took place at the Beacon Theatre in New York as a revival benefit for that theatre, with Princess Grace in attendance. The following day the film opened commercially to critical acclaim, and it later received an Academy Award nomination in the feature documentary category. In addition, *The Children of Theatre Street* was invited to be shown at the Cannes, San Francisco, Teheran, and Vancouver film festivals and given premieres in London and Paris. In Paris we were advised that it was only the second film in history to be celebrated at the Paris Opera House. But, most important, *The Children of Theatre Street* has raised and will continue to raise consciousnesses and contributions for ballet schools and companies across America.

Earle Mack
Producer and Co-director,
The Children of Theatre Street

1.

A School of Dancing is Founded

Classic ballet. Even to the layman those words bring to mind such names as Pavlova and Nijinsky. Today the dancers Rudolf Nureyev, Mikhail Baryshnikov, Natalia Makarova, and Valery Panov are celebrated in the West, and virtually guarantee full houses whenever they appear on stage. In the Soviet Union, Galina Ulanova, Marina Semeonova, Vakhtang Chabukiani, Konstantin Sergeyev, and Natalia Dudinskaya are already legends in their lifetime. And what do they all have in common? Apart from the fact that they have all ascended to the pinnacle of their art, each one is a graduate of the world's most famous dance academy. Now it is known as the Vaganova Choreographic Institute, but once it bore the simpler title the Imperial School of Ballet.

The history of the school is long, complex, and turbulent. But outside events that have changed the course of history have only temporarily disrupted the school's flow of activity. Its single-minded business is and always has been to produce the most beautifully trained dancers in the world. This commitment has been as constant as the White Nights that yearly illuminate Peter the Great's noble city.

Peter's "lofty thoughts" for a city to be built "on the mossy, marshy banks" facing the Gulf of Finland began to be realized in 1703, and the vast northlands of Russia, which were to be the site of Peter's "window on Europe," soon echoed to the sounds of the building of the new capital. Thousands of workers, peasants, soldiers, and craftsmen, brought in from all over Russia, toiled to build the palaces, the factories, the shipyards. At great cost of life, one of the most beautiful cities in the world, St. Petersburg, arose. Architects arrived from Europe to work with talented Russian designers. Palaces of incomparable elegance, cathedrals and churches whose spires and golden domes broke through the skyline, graceful bridges over serene canals, magnificent parks, and the lace patterns of the beautiful iron railings all basked under the clear northern light that gives St. Petersburg much of its individuality.

A wild but brilliant man, endowed with enormous gifts, Peter was fascinated all his life by Western culture. Undoubtedly it was the Westernization he inaugurated that was responsible for the founding, thirty-five years after the birth of St. Petersburg, of the Imperial School of Ballet.

In the century following the founding of St. Petersburg many talented Russian architects emerged. Among them was Carlo Rossi, who was born in Russia in 1775 to the Italian ballerina Gertrude Rossi, whose second husband was the dancer Charles Le Picq. Rossi studied in Italy for two years and returned to St. Petersburg in 1812. Sometime between 1828 and 1832 the ensemble of buildings that now houses the Vaganova Choreographic Institute was built according to his design. The street on which these buildings stand is now officially named Rossi Street, after its architect, but perhaps it will always be thought of as Theatre Street, a name made famous throughout the world by the unforgettable autobiography of Tamara Karsavina. She took Theatre Street as the title for this account of her childhood, her years at the theatre school, and her career in Russia up to her departure in 1918.

Marina Semeonova

Like so many of the buildings Rossi designed, Theatre Street is exquisitely conceived, composed of arches and columns, yellow and white in coloring, in the neo-classic style. The school and the dance archives are housed on the right side of the street as one looks toward the back of the Pushkin Theatre (formerly the Alexandrinsky Theatre). On the left side are the architectural offices. At the other end of the street facing the Pushkin Theatre is Lomonsov Square, and behind that is the Fontanka Canal. In this quiet, elegantly proportioned street, behind a façade so harmonious, so perfect, that it resembles a stage decor, frightened little girls have become great ballerinas and homesick boys have grown up to become world-famous choreographers.

*B*ut the story begins long before Theatre Street was built. Russian folk dance had for centuries played an important part in the daily lives of the peasants and ordinary people of Russia, but it was not until 1673 that the court dancing so popular in Europe was introduced to the Russian court. The summer palace of the Tsar Alexis, a quiet, pious youth who was known as "the gentle," was the site of the first ballet performance in Russia. The festivities, based on an interminable Greek myth, lasted more than ten hours. Alexis was so fired with enthusiasm, he decreed that a theatrical school be established in Moscow. Unfortunately, the dancers were poorly treated, badly fed, paid appallingly meager salaries, and the school lasted just three years.

But masquerades and balls introducing dances of the period continued to be popular in court circles. During the first quarter of the eighteenth century, when Peter the Great was at the height of his power (and St. Petersburg had replaced Moscow as the capital of Russia), assemblies and balls continued to flourish, and in a further effort to Westernize St. Petersburg society, Peter encouraged, even bullied, the wealthy aristocracy into dressing in the latest fashions from the West. Women were ordered to leave their cloistered homes and take their places in society, while the boyars were forced to shave off their beards.

These social reforms were not always popular. Nor were the taxes Peter imposed on the Russian people to pay for his wars and other ambitious projects. But despite the harshness of his methods, Peter's enormous energy and drive, his unyielding determination to make Russia a European power to be reckoned with, more than justify his place in history as the founder of modern Russia.

In 1730 Anna Ivanovna, niece of Peter the Great, became Empress of Russia. She was said to be an uneducated, uncouth person who found pleasure in crude jokes. Frantically pro-German, she was all her life under the influence of her favorite courtier, Johan Biron, one of the Baltic Germans who dominated her court. Because of his—or perhaps because of her own—interest in Russian folk dance, in 1734 Anna sent for a French ballet master to teach social dancing to the cadets of the Shliakhetny Corps.

Jean Baptiste Landé arrived on August 1, 1734, and immediately set to work. Impressed by the divertissement staged for the Corps des Cadets in an opera presented on January 29, 1736, Empress Anna agreed to Landé's request that he be allowed to form a school of dancing. On May 15, 1738, the school was officially opened.

Shortly after his arrival in Russia Landé had spotted some peasant children dancing on the quay and had been greatly taken with their charm and natural expressiveness. For this reason he requested that his pupils be selected from the poorer classes rather than from the aristocracy. Twelve boys and twelve girls were selected from among the children of palace servants. The children were given quarters in the Winter Palace, where Landé and his wife also lived, in a separate wing. A court groom became the assistant supervisor in charge of the children's educational needs.

Landé was asked "to give instructions to the young people in his charge, to teach them with sincerity, seriousness and all the qualities of a good man." All this he accomplished, and in addition to the art of the dance he taught his pupils the principles of choreography. The course itself was three years long, and at the end of that period a dancer was deemed sufficiently trained to perform professionally in the entertainments arranged for the court.

Anna did not live to see the fruits of Landé's efforts. She died in 1740, and was succeeded by Elizabeth, the favorite daughter of Peter the Great.

Blond, buxom, and very pretty, Elizabeth was loved by the court. In contrast to her unpopular predecessor, she spoke fluent French, and had a love of luxury. At her coronation in Moscow in 1742 a ballet with an allegorical theme typical of the day was performed by dancers from the St. Petersburg School. The choreographer was Antonio Fusano, who had arrived in St. Petersburg during Anna's reign and had actually given the young Elizabeth dancing lessons. (The new Empress was a most accomplished dancer.)

Fusano, with Landé, played a critical part in the training of the first young Russian dancers. As soon as foreigners heard of the school and of the interest of the Russian court in this art form, they came to St. Petersburg in large numbers to perform and teach, but the native-born dancers were quick to learn and were soon able to hold their own. During his period as a teacher in St. Petersburg Fusano added to Russian technique by introducing a greater range of beaten steps and showing the dancers new ways to improve their elevation. When Landé died, in 1745, Fusano inevitably assumed direction of the school. In 1756, yet another foreigner, the Italian Giovanni Locatelli, arrived in St. Petersburg with a company of opera singers and dancers.

Locatelli's work was much admired, and at Elizabeth's request he took over the opera house adjoining the Summer Garden. Here anyone in the city who had the money could buy a ticket for a performance. Locatelli's company was called the Italian Free Theatre, to indicate the difference between it and the Court Theatre, which admitted only the retinue of the Imperial family.

An Austrian ballet master, Frantz Hilferding van Weven, who was destined to wield enormous influence during the early years of ballet in Russia, arrived in 1759. Word of his achievements abroad and his reputation as an innovative choreographer reached the ears of the Empress Elizabeth, and she asked Empress Maria Theresa in Vienna to release Hilferding from his duties so that he might take up residence in St. Petersburg as ballet master to the Imperial School. The Austrian Empress, eager to find favor with Elizabeth, agreed, and Hilferding arrived at the Imperial School "to perfect ballet in St. Petersburg and to introduce new elements."

Among Hilferding's innovations in ballet were the introduction of mime, the abolishment of masks, and the addition of increased subject matter. Allegorical ballets and myths remained popular, but he also produced comedies and divertissements containing folk dances. Hilferding encouraged native talent and more and more Russian dancers appeared alongside the foreigners. Nevertheless, court circles still looked to the West for culture, and ballet masters and dancers continued to be sought abroad.

One of Hilferding's most prominent pupils was Timofei Seminovich Boublikov. Once a serf dancer, Boublikov became the first Russian premier danseur, sufficiently well thought of to be sent to Vienna in 1764 to gain further study. There he performed with considerable success in ballets by Gaspara Angiolini and Jean Georges Noverre before returning to Russia in 1765.

Boublikov was just one of many serf dancers, albeit among the most distinguished. During Catherine the Great's reign many noblemen and landowners of enormous wealth retained on their estates dancers, singers, and musicians who were beckoned to entertain at the whim of their masters. When not engaged in the business of performing, the serfs were expected to do menial work in the fields or household.

Serf dancers were often sold by their masters to the Imperial theatres. Some were sent at Imperial expense to the theatre school in St. Petersburg or Moscow for further training, and then bought back again by their masters. Large sums of money changed hands for this purpose.

If they were young and attractive, serf dancers might be pampered and protected. Others were less fortunate. Yuri Slonimsky, the eminent Soviet dance historian, has written, "Many of them died without having had the chance to blossom, some drowned their unhappy lot in wine."

This era of "nameless tragedies, buried talents and premature deaths" lingered until 1806, when the last group of scrf dancers was bought by the Imperial Theatre in Moscow. It was not, however, until 1824 that a law was passed by Alexander I freeing the serfs dancing in Imperial theatres, and the serfs throughout Russia were not freed until 1861, two years before slavery was abolished in the United States.

Throughout this period of trading in dancers the students of the Imperial Theatre were comparatively well cared for and the school itself became well known as a training ground. An extremely important factor was the 1762 order of Catherine II creating a new position intended to reorganize the theatres in Moscow and St. Petersburg. The director of the Imperial theatres would have charge of opera, drama, and ballet, as well as responsibility for the schools. Ivan P. Yelagin was the first to be entrusted with this position. From 1766 until 1917, the year of the Russian Revolution, the director of the Imperial theatres and the committee under him had responsibility for all major decisions, but it was the court and the Imperial dynasty that wielded the influence and the Imperial treasury that paid the bills.

*I*n 1766, the same year that Catherine created the position of director of the Imperial theatres, she sent for a pupil of Hilferding's in Vienna, Gasparo Angiolini. Once again a foreigner was to exert tremendous influence on Russian ballet. Angiolini, a fervent disciple of Hilferding, remained loyal to him and to his teachings. Four years older than the famed Noverre, Angiolini was his bitter opponent because he felt that Noverre had claimed as his own innovations that rightfully belonged to Hilferding. Angiolini also believed that Noverre's work was overly intellectual and insufficiently balletic. A brilliant and inventive choreographer who was in many respects ahead of his time, Angiolini traveled frequently but returned regularly to St. Petersburg to teach at the school and to carry on with the work of Hilferding.

It was during Angiolini's time at the theatre school that Yelagin was replaced as director. The new man in charge set about reorganizing the School of Ballet, joining it with the existing schools of Music and Art. Additional teachers were brought in, and art, music, elocution, Russian, French, and Italian were added to the curriculum. In three years Catherine found a new director and committee, and once again the schools were reorganized. This was a disastrous period for Russian ballet. The newcomers had little knowledge of the theatre and still less of the training of dancers.

The new committee took an interest in the school, particularly in its enchanting female pupils. The improvements could undoubtedly be attributed to the nonacademic interest excited by the young girls. The food provided the students was better in quality, and the clothing allotted to them also improved. At this time the students were being increasingly courted by the nobility, not least among them the director of the Imperial Theatre himself. Nevertheless, it did not always pay to "intrigue with Her Majesty's foster children." Yelagin and his successor had both been dismissed for such peccadillos.

*I*n 1785 the school moved once more, this time to the house of a nobleman in Litany Street.

The new director, Major General Soymonov, had some advanced ideas. One of them, still carried out at the Vaganova Choreographic Institute, was the "Trial Evenings." On these occasions the students would perform before their ballet masters so that their progress could be assessed. In this way it could be discovered which of the students should be encouraged, which should be goaded into making greater efforts, and which should be directed toward other careers. The new director was lucky enough to have an excellent new ballet master, Joseph Canziani, to help him carry out his plans. Canziani, a teacher at the school, had replaced Angiolini when he left St. Petersburg for the final time in 1786, and he was well rewarded by an unusually high salary upon his promotion to ballet master.

Unlike Angiolini, Canziani was an ardent follower of Noverre's principles. A contemporary account records that "He paid great attention to mime and tried to throw off from the faces of his pupils the set expressions—the 'masks'—which earlier they had been taught to wear on stage."

In a letter to Voltaire, written in 1763, Noverre summed up his own credo: "For over six years I have tried to give a new form to the dance. I have felt that it is possible to render poems as ballets. I have abandoned symmetrical figures. I have joined to the mechanical movements of feet and arms the movements of the soul and the varied expressions of the face. I have got rid of masks, I have pledged myself to the use of costumes that are truer and more in style." In Noverre's opinion, "The hands of the capable dancer must be able to speak; if his face is not expressive, if his eyes are not eloquent, then everything is without meaning, everything is mechanical." It was also Noverre's strong belief that subject matter must be chosen so as to be intelligible to audiences through dancing.

Canziani, a prolific choreographer, persevered at the school until 1792, when he left in disgust at the way Prince Yusupov, appointed director the year before, was administering the affairs of the school. Yusupov had appointed a school superintendent, who took it upon himself to alter drastically the schedule and maintenance of the school. The changes were so extreme that by the end of the eighteenth century only seven names were listed specifically as students of dance, many dance students having been forced into dramatic acting or other theatrical professions. No wonder Canziani left. Yusupov agreed to all of the radical changes.

Canziani's pupil, Ivan Valberkh, who taught at the school beginning in 1794, succeeded him as principal ballet master. He was fortunate enough to have in St. Petersburg one of the most illustrious dancers of the day: Charles Le Picq, a pupil of Noverre's. Although Le Picq was famed as a dancer, his reputation in Russia was principally as a ballet master and teacher. (To Le Picq later went the credit for ensuring that Noverre's famous *Lettres sur la Danse* was published in Russia. In 1803 the French edition came out in four volumes at Alexander I's expense. Noverre's principles and reforms were eagerly taken up in Russia by many who had never seen him but whom he greatly influenced.)

The son of a theatrical tailor to the Imperial theatres, Valberkh had graduated from the school in 1786. He appears to have been a somewhat controversial figure, but he was the first Russian-born ballet master to graduate from the theatre school, and he did well enough to be sent to Europe for advanced study in 1801. Valberkh has variously been referred to in contemporary accounts as a "man of the theatre" and a "half-baked ballet master." Upon his return from Europe he created many ballets, often with fervently patriotic or anti-Napoleonic themes. He also created domestic Russian ballets and works he referred to as "ballets of morals," including his best-known ballet, *Werther*, which was based on Goethe's novel.

However, Valberkh's years as ballet master of the St. Petersburg School and inspector of the ballet company were among the worst in the school's history, partly because of the continuing inadequacies of Yusupov, whose knowledge of dance appears to have been minimal, and also the influence of Tsar Paul.

In 1798 the eccentric, despotic Tsar invited to St. Petersburg a new ballet master, Peicam de Chevalier-Bressolles. There was no artistic motive behind the invitation; rather, it was extended to please an influential courtier, Count Kutaisov, who was the lover of Chevalier's wife, an actress of rare and renowned beauty. The inept new ballet master was officially designated by Tsar Paul as "ballet composer for life," but he lasted only three years in Russia. He choreographed at least a dozen ballets, most of them reputedly very bad, and became a laughingstock to all but the Tsar. Paul had a passion for military formations and marches and Chevalier filled his ballets with them.

It was during Chevalier's tenure that male performers were banned by order of the Tsar, who intensely disliked the spectacle of men dancing. Consequently, male roles were performed *en travesti* by female dancers. Many renowned foreign dancers were dismissed from the company, and the women who remained were forced to attend guards' parades, presumably to increase their efficiency in the military-style ballets that were put on to satisfy Paul's obsession. No expenses were spared on the productions, so long as Chevalier indulged Paul's whims.

One good thing did come out of this sorry period. Madame Chevalier-Bressolles' brother, Auguste Poirot, a superb dancer, choreographer, and teacher, remained to give thirty years of dedicated service to his newfound and passionately loved land. Auguste, as he was always known, was very handsome and loved by everyone. A marvelous demi-caractère dancer, his influence made Russian folk dance fashionable, not only in the theatre but also in high social circles.

*J*ust months before his death Tsar Paul heard of the success a certain Charles Louis Didelot was having in London. He instructed the recently appointed director of the Imperial theatres, Alexander Naryshkin, to invite Didelot to join the company as ballet master and premier danseur, and also to teach at the theatre school. Didelot accepted and arrived soon after Paul was assassinated that year.

The first few months were trying ones for Didelot. Since he came so soon after Chevalier, the dancers naturally suspected that he was similarly corrupt. They need not have worried. With the help of Valberkh (before his departure later that year for Europe), Le Picq, and Auguste, Didelot set to work immediately to reorganize the school. The vast and varied experience he had gained in Stockholm, London, and Copenhagen, where he had worked with the leading ballet personalities of the day, Auguste and Gaetan Vestris and Jean Dauberval, stood him in excellent stead. Before long Didelot had brought the Imperial Ballet School into line with the best training in Europe. One of his first moves was to increase Valberkh's "two quiet hours" of dance training to four or five hours a day. Mime became an increasingly important part of the curriculum, for Didelot, like Noverre, considered drama one of the most important elements of dance.

The school benefited almost immediately from Didelot's influence, particularly since a muscular injury in 1805 hindered his dancing for several years. Since he found it painful to perform, Didelot devoted more time to improving the teaching conditions at the school, which by the year of his injury had nearly tripled its initial enrollment.

Obviously there was a need for larger and better accommodations (the building the school was housed in appeared to be near collapse). In 1805 new and improved quarters were found in a three-story building overlooking the Ofitsersky and Ekaterinsky (now named Griboyedov) canals. Soon after, a small church was built convenient to the new quarters in an effort to safeguard the morals of the pupils. "Dancers may be dancers but belief in God must not be shaken" was the pious opinion of their elders.

Didelot showed himself to be highly industrious and dedicated. In his twenty-seven years in Russia he produced more than fifty ballets, and among his most important innovations was invisible stage machinery that enabled him to create magical effects. These continued to be popular right through the period of Romantic ballet.

In addition to his stage inventions, his solid craftsmanship also won him the admiration of his audience. Didelot's style of choreography varied according to the type of dance he was creating. Fluid and graceful movements were created for his principal performers, but he delighted also in giving them beautiful poses and attitudes. He avoided the use of entrechats and pirouettes except in demi-caractère dances, which he customarily set to allegro music, giving performers swift movements of the feet and arms, which contrasted with those movements used by his principals. His humorous dances were different once again, often built on jumps and turns in the air. This individuality of approach was a key mark of the Didelot style, for he believed that steps should have different emphasis according to the differing moods of the ballet. He insisted on purity of style, a trait that he himself had markedly possessed as a performer.

Didelot coached and taught hundreds of dancers during his years in St. Petersburg, and many of them graduated to achieve high honors for themselves and for their teacher. Didelot believed that "one must spend a large part of one's day in reading historical books, extracting subjects from them for future compositions." The early morning was set aside for this, after which Didelot would make sketches of the choreographic groupings for which he was famed, the required costumes, and even the necessary props. Then he would proceed to the ballet school, arriving to conduct class at about eleven o'clock, "wearing a short brown frock coat, unfastened, with no vest. A great white collar, almost reaching to his ears, was set off by a bright scarf around his neck. While a violin played, an elm baton in his hand tapped the cadence as the students did their endless battements and ronds des jambes."

Much has been written about Didelot by his pupils. The accounts provide vivid insights into Didelot's temperament:

Didelot was an extraordinary sight when he watched the dancers on the stage from the wings. He minced and smiled, performed little steps where he stood, then suddenly lost his temper and beat his foot violently on the ground. When the dancers were children, he shook his fist at them, and woe betide them if they ever made mistakes in forming groups. He pounced on them like a vulture, caught them by one ear or by the hair, and when they struggled, he gave them a generous dose of kicks which made them vanish as quickly as they could. Even the soloists were sometimes punished. Under a burst of applause the dancer would withdraw into the wings. Didelot was watching for her there, he grabbed her by the shoulders, shook her like a plum tree, showered her with insults and with a thump on the back shoved her back on the stage to take another bow. Often he could be seen running in the wings after some victim who thought to escape him. When he was in a real temper it took a shower of water to bring him back to his senses.

Another of Didelot's pupils recalls that "the greater his interest in one particular pupil, the more 'attention' was lavished on her. Often you could pick out a coming star by the bruises which she had. The slightest mistake was rewarded with a blow, a slap, or a thump."

After several hours of teaching the pupils all manner of dance technique, Didelot would leave for the theatre to supervise rehearsals of his ballets. After a hurried dinner, he would once more make his way to the theatre for the evening performance. It was a long and exhausting day, but Didelot's efforts began to pay off.

The outstanding graduates during Didelot's early years as a teacher in Russia were Maria Ikonina, Anastasia Novitskaya, Maria Danilova, and Adam Glushkovsky. Ikonina was regarded as a strong and precise technician, but some found her a cold dancer. Novitskaya, on the other hand, was praised by contemporary critics for her "tenderness and modesty, nobility and charm." Her dancing was said to have "inexpressible lightness and purity." A year after that accolade, in 1810, the seventeen-year-old Danilova was officially graduated.

Maria Danilova had performed off and on in public since childhood, for her talent was extraordinary. So extraordinary, in fact, that in 1837 one critic who had just seen the legendary Taglioni for the first time was prompted to remember:

There was a time when our theatre had its own Russian Taglioni . . . when only the appearance of this enchantress brought rapture to the public. This Taglioni, like the former, was called Maria, but she was Russian, ours at heart and in origin. She grew up under our stern sky, on our cold shores, but with a soul of fire. Young, beautiful and charming, she flashed in our theatre like a poet's dream.

Danilova had been placed with intelligent foresight in the theatre school by her parents at the age of eight. Once rich, they found themselves in greatly reduced circumstances, and the prospect of a free education for their pretty little daughter must have been appealing to them. She did not let them down. From the beginning Danilova was picked out to appear onstage in roles requiring talented children from the school, such as cupids and genies. Evgenia Kolosova, who had been a pupil of Valberkh's and the first major ballerina of Didelot's era, noticed the talented child and took a great interest in her. With the encouragement of Didelot, Kolosova set to work on the young artist, teaching her the art of mime, in which she herself excelled. Kolosova herself had been described by a critic as follows: "With the expressive lines of her face, beautiful figure and majestic bearing, Kolosova could speak by glances and movements better than by speech."

Didelot was aware of Danilova's special gifts, but he did not want to rush her. Instead he removed her from the public eye and continued polishing and refining her dancing. When as a very alluring young woman she reappeared onstage, she caused a sensation. Men flocked to her in an attempt to win her favor, but for all of them she had a ready answer: "I am not free; I belong to my art." This single-mindedness did not last long, for at the age of fifteen she fell head over heels in love with a visiting French dancer, the great Louis Duport.

An excellent technician, Duport has been variously described as "lithe as a rubber ball" and "light as a bird." It has been said that he was able to cross the stage in two leaps, and his pirouettes were done at such speed (performed always on the tips of his demi-point) that he seemed "like a well-built machine." Didelot, however, felt that Duport's brilliant dancing lacked "soul." (He also resented Duport for taking credit for Danilova's success as a dancer.)

Soon the French visitor fell out of favor. He returned to his fiancée and left Russia without even saying good-bye to the heartsick Danilova. She died only a few months later at the age of seventeen from tuberculosis. (And, some say, from a broken heart.) Her death occurred one year to the day after she had appeared as Psyche in the premiere of Didelot's ballet *Psyche et l'Amour*.

The best male dancer among Didelot's earliest graduates was Adam Glushkovsky, who became almost a son to Didelot. Didelot had taken young Adam into his family when he discovered that the child was homeless. Years later in his *Memoirs* Glushkovsky reminisced fondly about his childhood with Didelot and his wife Rose, who lived at the time in a wing of the vast and fortresslike Mikhailovsky Palace. Glushkovsky repaid Didelot's generosity by becoming one of the ballet master's most successful protégés.

The year 1809 brought considerable changes to the theatre school, whose enrollment—one hundred twenty pupils—had doubled since Didelot arrived. Tsar Alexander passed a law decreeing totally new rules for the school. The incompetents who had been responsible for the inefficient running of the building and the care of the pupils were replaced by entirely fresh personnel. Now entrance examinations became compulsory and were to be supervised by a doctor and a ballet master. In the future the pupils were to be divided into three divisions. The first would include students under the age of thirteen. In addition to their theatrical training (whether in areas of dance or theatre or both), they now had to study divinity, French, Russian, arithmetic, music, and art. The second division would consist of students from the age of thirteen to graduation. Academic subjects would be continued, but less time allotted to them. The main concentration would be on dance or theatre. The third division was reserved for the especially talented pupils who had shown particular brilliance in their chosen field. These studied solely the theatrical art to which they were now fully destined. A fourth division catered to those students who, after a few years' training, had not acquired the ability to become successful performers. These students were trained to work backstage in areas such as wardrobe or props.

In addition to the changes in staff and the restructuring of grades and entrance examinations, the decree determined rules for a code of behavior, for parents' visiting days, and for standardized attire. A weekly report on the students' all-around progress was another innovation.

The decree ordered that a performance be given every six months before the director of the Imperial theatres and other officials of the theatre. Prominent theatrical artists as well as certain students and relatives would also be permitted to attend, but not the general public. The performance would take place in the school theatre. This splendid practice is still in operation.

In issuing the new decree, the Tsar had been influenced by Didelot and by the dramatist Alexander A. Shakhovsky, who throughout his life took a great interest in the theatre school and even founded a Youth Theatre. Shakhovsky himself had an important position in the repertory department of the Imperial theatres, and saw to it that only persons of genuine talent and authentic theatrical education were employed as staff at the theatre school.

The new regime very soon justified itself. The school did suffer a slight relapse during the years 1811-1816. Didelot went abroad on leave of absence, but the quality of teaching picked up rapidly upon his return. Didelot's absence, however, had not affected the training of the first ballerina to emerge upon his return to Russia.

$\mathcal{A}$vdotia Istomina, who made her debut in 1815, has been immortalized in Pushkin's great poem *Eugene Onegin*. She received her training from the Russian teachers who remained at the school after Didelot's departure, but as a performer she owed almost everything to Didelot. She was his muse, his inspiration. Her graceful dancing caught the attention of the great writer Alexander Pushkin, who, like many of his friends, spent much time at the ballet. In Pushkin's words, Istomina was the "embodiment of the soul in flight." The dark-haired, dark-eyed Istomina was the cause of a duel between several of Pushkin's friends, in which one of them, who had been her lover, was killed. (When Pushkin was only thirty-seven years old, he too died of stomach wounds sustained in a duel over his wife.)

The young men of Pushkin's generation were fascinated by the beautiful girls who danced on the stages of St. Petersburg's theatres and found all sorts of ways to penetrate the backstage corridors and dressing rooms. Many ingenious methods, including disguises, were used to slip past the authorities in order to get near to their idols. It was somewhat easier to plan meetings once the girls joined the company, for then they were unchaperoned. Many of the young men, who were cadets and university students with plenty of money and influential connections, courted the young ballerinas with expensive gifts. The Soviet historian Yuri Slonimsky, in researching this period, discovered that Pushkin, while a student, took dancing classes, which possibly explains his knowledgeable interest and descriptive prose. Pushkin admired Didelot and mentions him in the verses of *Eugene Onegin:* "In all M. Didelot's ballets we find his hallmark—vivid imagination and boundless charm."

Didelot knew many of the leading writers and intellectuals of the day. One of them introduced him to Pushkin's poem *The Prisoner of the Caucasus*. It inspired Didelot to create in 1823 his last important ballet (of the same name), and Istomina, as the Circassian Girl, gave such a remarkable performance that she is still associated with the ballet. One hundred fifty years later Pushkin's winged words and vivid imagery continue to inspire choreographers.

$\mathcal{T}$he life of a ballet student in the 1820s was hard and exhausting. For the aspiring dancer, a typical winter's day would start in the early hours while the sky was still pitch black. At six o'clock practice would begin in the chilly, barely lit classrooms, and it continued until it was time for breakfast. Then followed more classes and more rehearsals. One of the few compensations for students at the theatre school and members of the Imperial Ballet was the luxury of being transported to and from the theatres in covered carriages. Warmly wrapped up against the cold night air, they were spared the tiring walk home after a long day's work.

Despite the glamour of performing before bejeweled audiences, ballet was an exhausting life for students and professionals alike, and they deserved their brief vacations in the palaces outside St. Petersburg. The grounds of Gatchina and Pavlovsk, with their lushly landscaped parks adorned with statues and fountains, were a haven for the enjoyment of the dancers. Here they could walk among the lakes and leafy greenery and renew their strength.

The Imperial dancers could also look forward to a pension paid out of the Imperial treasury at the end of their dancing careers. Many of the female dancers married into the aristocracy, but for those who did not make well-connected marriages a retirement pension gave hope and comfort.

Nevertheless, despite the advantages and bonuses, in comparison to foreigners Russian dancers were still often discriminated against in terms of salary and position. For example, the French dancer Duport, while a guest in St. Petersburg, received the incredibly high salary of 60,000 rubles, in comparison with the mere 7500 rubles paid to the lovely ballerina Kolosova. This disparity infuriated Didelot. Throughout his career he fought vigorously the injustice of unequal pay.

Another dancer whose Russian birth meant a constant struggle to obtain the same rights guest dancers took for granted was Nilolai Holtz, a pupil at the school from 1806 to 1822. It is not recorded why he should have taken so long to graduate, but Mary Grace Swift, in her biography of Didelot, *A Loftier Flight*, writes that "the directors liked to prolong the schooling of talented pupils because they could be used in performances without receiving performers' salaries." Holtz, when he did finally graduate, was the first male dancer to enter the company as a full-fledged soloist. He also received the singular honor of being cast in Didelot's *The Prisoner of the Caucasus* within a few months of entering the company. Fourteen years later it was Holtz, by now an established premier danseur, who was chosen to partner the great Marie Taglioni during her two hundred performances in Russia.

Holtz was described by Didelot as "an irreplaceable mime, an astonishing character dancer" who "proved the victim of his own integrity. This young man is like some useful plant, with a pliant bending stalk; without a murmur he suffers every kind of reprimand when he deserves nothing but praise." Later in his career Holtz took up teaching, and among his pupils was the composer Mikhail Glinka. In the mid-forties Holtz was asked by Glinka to choreograph a mazurka for use in *A Life for the Tsar*, later to become one of Glinka's most famous works. Holtz had an immensely long and successful career. In 1872 the Imperial Ballet celebrated fifty years of Holtz's performances on the stages of Russia.

The final years for Didelot were less happy. Always a proud and stubborn man, he found himself increasingly harassed by the director of the Imperial theatres, Prince Gagarin, who bitterly resented Didelot's arrogant, unbending attitude. Finally, in 1828, Didelot resigned in protest. His resignation was not accepted. For the next year and a half Didelot fought to have his name cleared. It was not until a benefit was given for him in October 1833 that the old man could feel partially vindicated. It was a heartwarming occasion, prompting a spontaneous demonstration of affection by the entire company—soloists, corps de ballet, and pupils of the Imperial School alike.

Despite this massive send-off, Didelot spent his final years bereft of his beloved pupils, in loneliness and failing health. The "father of Russian ballet" was finally persuaded by his doctor to visit sunnier climes to improve his health. In 1836 he departed for Kiev. En route he passed through Moscow to visit his former pupil, Adam Glushkovsky, now ballet master at the Imperial Theatre in Moscow, and was immensely touched to see hanging on a wall a portrait of himself, evidence that he had not been forgotten. While in Moscow he took the opportunity to visit the historical sites of the former capital. An avid reader all his life, he was familiar with the background of them all.

Didelot left his mark on Russian ballet in many ways, but it was as a teacher of dancing at the theatre school that he is perhaps best remembered. His inspired coaching and his wholehearted love for his pupils profoundly affected generations of Russian dancers. "Didelot was unpredictable, often unbearable and made many enemies in high places, but those who knew him and profited from his teachings loved him and worshipped him," wrote one of his pupils.

The final gesture of the old ballet master was typical: when he died, in 1837, he left all his money to the school of the Imperial Ballet to found scholarships for future students.

After Didelot's departure Russian ballet passed through a few barren years. New teachers were brought into the theatre school, but there was nobody with anything like Didelot's authority and dedication.

Nevertheless the theatre school continued undaunted. If not inspired, at least the training continued and dance classes remained the focal point of the day for the young students. The administration underwent yet another change in 1835 when a new director, Alexander Gedeonov, was appointed.

Unlike his predecessor, Gagarin, who never consorted with the female dancers, Gedeonov had distinct favorites. This did not stop him from lecturing the dancers when Anastasia Novitskaya wished to marry. "My children, you know nothing of life. And yet what do I hear? Why, that one of you wishes to be married—and to an actor! What are his means? Have you a dowry? No! Then what are you going to live on? In a year's time you will have children and be unable to dance for several months, and so you will remain all your life in the corps de ballet. I really feel sorry for you."

Gedeonov's warnings did not prevent romantic assignations. The pupils lived on the top floor of the three-story house on the Ekaterinsky Canal, and it was not uncommon for balletomanes and students to attempt to attract their attention from the street below. Nor was it uncommon for them to wait for the dancers when they returned home from the theatre. Because the suitors were often well connected, the authorities usually preferred to turn a blind eye to any liaisons that were formed.

When the school moved in 1835 to the street designed by Rossi behind the Alexandrinsky Theatre, the ballet pupils found themselves accommodated on the first floor of the five-floor building, but the windows were glazed over to prevent those inside from seeing out.

𝒲hile St. Petersburg dance activity was sadly humdrum, the capitals of Europe buzzed with talk of the great Romantic ballerina Marie Taglioni. In 1832 her father, Filippo Taglioni, had choreographed the ideal role for her in a ballet that was the very epitome of Romanticism—the Sylph in *La Sylphide*. Wherever Taglioni appeared in the new ballet she created a sensation. Russia was not to see her or *La Sylphide* until 1837, but when that day finally arrived the public's lagging interest in ballet was instantly revived.

At the age of thirty-three, at the very peak of her career, Taglioni "surpassed our wildest dreams," wrote one critic. "She danced like a goddess not on, but rather over, the stage," wrote another. Taglioni visited St. Petersburg at the demand of the public for five years running, arriving in September and remaining in Russia until February.

Tsar Nicholas I was so bewitched by Taglioni that he rarely missed one of her performances, and at his command a statue of the great dancer was placed in the Royal Box. He presented her with frequent gifts, including an ermine cape. On one occasion the Tsar, breaking with precedent, left his own seat for one in the front row of the orchestra stalls, in order to observe his idol more closely. Always a great enthusiast of the ballet, Tsar Nicholas apparently had a mistress who was a dancer and frequently showed his sympathetic interest in the art by coming to the assistance of ballet when funds were low. He was often seen backstage and visited the Imperial Ballet School at least once a year. On one occasion he was overheard to say, "Even my dogs lead a better life than these dear little things." In view of the opulence of life at the Imperial Court in the mid-nineteenth century, the Tsar was almost certainly not joking.

𝒮t. Petersburg was a highly fashionable city in the 1840s, when Taglioni fever was at its height. The Tsar's court was composed of hundreds of well-connected aristocrats, guards officers, intellectuals, foreigners, and dilettantes who, along with the Tsar himself, demanded the latest in literature, music, art, and theatre. Much of it still came from Europe, but Russia by now was developing her own culture. Writers, painters, playwrights, and composers with a distinct Russian view of life were making St. Petersburg and Moscow aware of their abilities.

The children of Theatre Street, surrounded by elegance and riches, continued to live uncomplicated lives dedicated to the pursuit of their art. Although they frequently performed in the ballets staged at the opera houses, they were always carefully chaperoned and bundled hastily into coaches at the end of a performance. Sometimes the aspiring young dancers would go to the theatre not to dance but to watch and learn. On these occasions they would sit demurely in the third-ring boxes, causing almost as much interest as the performance itself. Eager balletomanes would turn their opera glasses on the faces of the young girls sitting in their light-blue dresses and white capes and pick out future stars and identify favorites.

The same year that Taglioni made her debut in Russia, two exceptionally fine dancers graduated from the theatre school, dividing St. Petersburg balletomanes into different camps. They were Elena Andreyanova and Tatiana Smirnova. Both learned much from Taglioni and both were often later compared to her. In years to come their dancing was considered comparable to that of the European dancers who succeeded Taglioni. And there were many. Fanny Elssler, Carlotta Grisi, Lucille Grahn, Fanny Cerrito—all the great Romantic ballerinas found their way to Russia, the exotic country with astonishing ballet companies and knowledgeable and receptive audiences. By now the two Imperial companies in St. Petersburg and Moscow could stand comparison with any in Europe. Though international stars were still warmly welcomed, it became clear that they were no longer essential to the well-being of the Russian ballet. The dancers who were being graduated from the theatre schools had technique, style, and a particularly Russian allure, compounded of the dramatic quality inherent in Russians and their special "soul."

Elena Andreyanova became the first Russian interpreter of *Giselle* in 1842, and later danced the role with distinction in Paris, Milan, and London. She also had the distinction of being chosen as the partner of Christian Johansson when he arrived to dance in St. Petersburg on May 31, 1841, and Marius Petipa when he arrived six years later. For a little more than a decade Andreyanova graced the stages of Russia and Europe, in competition with the leading European dancers of the day.

Smirnova, who had studied in her early youth with Didelot, proved an equal favorite with the public. She inherited many of Taglioni's roles, proving especially well suited to them because of her extreme lightness, delicacy of movement, and modesty of manner. Judging from contemporary accounts discovered by the historian Cyril Beaumont, Andreyanova was something of a schemer, and Smirnova sometimes suffered as a consequence. As Gedeonov's favorite, Andreyanova had ballets created for her, whereas the more retiring Smirnova did not.

Romantic ballet was still riding a crest of popularity when Jules Perrot arrived in St. Petersburg in 1848. Perrot, one of the greatest choreographers of the nineteenth century, spent a little more than a decade in Russia, where he introduced new trends and ideas. Though very much a Romantic choreographer, he moved ballet away from the gossamer images to which audiences everywhere had grown accustomed. Perrot's ballets in the 1850s were about real people rather than elusive spirits. Villains as well as heroes took center stage. The leading characters had dramatic depths and his stories blazed with conviction. Just as the composer Alberto Cavos had proved an invaluable collaborator for Didelot, so Perrot found his ideal collaborator in the Italian Cesare Pugni. The two created many ballets together.

Perrot's ballets were brought to life by many dancers, but particularly by one of the greatest ballerinas of the Romantic period and Taglioni's main rival, the exquisite Viennese Fanny Elssler. One critic comparing the two dancers wrote, "Taglioni symbolizes the ether; Elssler, earth mingled with fire." Elssler on stage was beautiful and womanly, unlike the ethereal Taglioni. She was particularly successful in such ballets as Perrot's *Esmeralda* and Dauberval's *La Fille Mal Gardée*. Her interpretation of the character solo *La Cacucha* was adored by ballet audiences. In this solo she was able to display the most remarkable passion and vitality.

Elssler took a great interest in the ballet school during her time in St. Petersburg, and on one of her visits she picked out the young Marfa Mouravieva, daughter of a serf, and predicted for her an important career. "She will succeed me," declared Elssler, after seeing the ten-year-old Mouravieva dance the role of Cupid in a ballet staged by Elssler herself.

Perrot was once described by Gautier as "the male Taglioni," despite his "extremely ugly" appearance. Bournonville, a classmate of Perrot's, seemed to support this view, for he recounts in his memoirs Vestris's instructions to him: "Never stay still—jump, leap, turn, pirouette, fly away, and above all never give the public time to study your features." Perrot, "a zephyr with the wings of a bat," was undoubtedly a formidable virtuoso, but he is remembered more for his achievements as the co-choreographer of *Giselle* than as a dancer.

The last thirty years of Perrot's life were spent in virtual retirement in France, with only the occasional dancer dropping by for private coaching in one of his roles. Dried up creatively, Perrot produced nothing after his departure from St. Petersburg in 1861. Perhaps his last years in Russia were a misery because of the churlish treatment meted out to him by the theatre officials, who were appalled by the democratic tendencies evident in his ballet librettos and who insisted upon making changes in them. Disillusioned, Perrot left, never to return.

Arthur Saint-Léon, Perrot's successor, was a different type of individual. During the decade he spent as ballet master in St. Petersburg he was perfectly happy to cater to public taste and bend to Imperial preferences. During his tenure he brought to the Russian stage ballets of much spectacle but little substance. At best they were entertaining and well crafted, even innovative in some respects. *The Little Hump-backed*

Horse, for example, emphasized with great success Russian folk dance and rural life, and its colorful visual effects proved admirably suited to the taste of the time. Later still he contributed *Coppélia*, again emphasizing the integration of folk dance into the structure.

The little girl picked out by Elssler, Marfa Mouravieva, later became Saint-Léon's favorite ballerina. She performed the ballerina roles in many of Saint-Léon's ballets, including the role of the Tsar Maiden in *The Little Hump-backed Horse*. Sadly, Mouravieva was forced to retire at the height of her fame and talent when she married a wealthy aristocrat at the age of twenty-seven. Fourteen years later she died of consumption. Her husband, whose mother had urged Mouravieva to cut short her career, bequeathed a large sum of money to the theatre school after her death to be used for a scholarship in memory of his beloved wife.

During the first years of its existence the ballet in St. Petersburg was influenced by many great ballet masters from Europe who enriched the repertory and improved the standards of dancing. There can be little doubt that Didelot was the dominant figure during the first part of the nineteenth century, and just as certainly Marius Petipa, also from France, towered over Russian ballet in the final years of that century.

Petipa arrived in Russia on May 24, 1847, at the invitation of the current ballet master of the Imperial Ballet, Antoine Dauchy Titus. Though his initial contract was just for a year, he remained in Russia for the rest of his life. He lived through the reigns of four Tsars and through a period of ballet that ranged from the flowering of the Romantic image to the birth of a new century and a wholly different concept of choreography.

Petipa's father, Jean, had preceded Marius to St. Petersburg, and when Petipa arrived, his father was already giving classes to the boys of the theatre school as well as performing certain character roles in the company. Petipa, however, had come to Russia primarily to dance, and early on he was seen in the ballets of Perrot and Saint-Leon with the leading ballerinas of the Imperial Ballet, Andreyanova and Smirnova, as well as the great Fanny Elssler. Within months of his arrival Petipa had begun to teach as well as to choreograph. He restaged with success two of Joseph Mazilier's most popular ballets, *Paquita* and *Satinella*, and continued to show an interest in choreography, producing several works for the company. It was some years, however, before Petipa had an undisputed triumph. This came in 1862 with *Daughter of Pharaoh*, choreographed with the guest ballerina Carolina Rosati in the leading role. Officially, Petipa staged the ballet in the brief space of six weeks, although it had been in secret preparation for two years while Petipa awaited an opportunity to produce it.

In 1855 Petipa had been appointed instructor at the theatre school, where he specialized in the coaching of mime. The year before that he had married Marie Sarovschikova, a recent graduate of the school. For the next few years, and until their separation in 1867, Petipa choreographed many ballets displaying Marie's qualities. He considered her "the most graceful of all dancers with the body of a Venus" and exploited her acting ability and very considerable charm in many ballets. The Petipas' daughter Maria, born in 1857, also became a dancer.

When Saint-Léon left St. Petersburg to return to Paris, in 1869, Petipa realized his ambition of becoming ballet-master-in-chief of the Imperial theatres in St. Petersburg and Moscow. The job carried with it full responsibility for the theatre school. Freed at last from the inhibiting presence of Saint-Léon, Petipa was now able to discover his individual and sparkling choreographic style. His earlier attempts had sometimes been judged derivative, even though his potential was evident from the beginning. Despite the uphill struggle to establish himself as a choreographer, Petipa's ambition had never faltered. The 1870s presented problems for the new ballet master, however. Public interest in the ballet was at an ebb, and male dancing was practically nonexistent and soon to become a thing of distant memory.

Earlier, in 1858, Théophile Gautier visited the theatre school and wrote,

Their conservatory of the dance possesses soloists and a corps de ballet which know no equal in harmony, precision, and swiftness of evolution. It gives one a rare satisfaction to watch those lines, so straight, those groups, so well defined, which break up only at precise moments to assume some new form, at those legs moving to the rhythm of the dance, at all those choreographic battalions who never become confused in their movements and never lose their way in their manoeuvres. All so young, so beautifully built, so perfectly well trained in their profession or in their art, if you prefer.

However, now the other critics were not so kind: "The corps de ballet dances carelessly, drags its feet, hardly moves its arms, tramples upon the stage. . . ." "Our corps de ballet is not being freshened up with new faces and girl pupils are allowed to push themselves up from the school directly into the ranks of soloists." Dancers were accused of missing their daily classes, and the paucity of male dancers was noted with the comment, "In nearly thirty years the school has not graduated a single premier danseur." The three male dancers (none of them young) who were still performing in the 1870s were Lev Ivanov, Pavel Gerdt, and Christian Johansson, who had arrived from Sweden in 1841. In Paris the shortage of male dancers had resulted in women being called upon to play male roles *en travesti*. So far this desperate state of affairs had been avoided on Russian stages.

Petipa, inspired choreographer that he was, fought against the widespread inertia. In 1869 he was summoned to Moscow, where he choreographed the Spanish-flavored *Don Quixote*, based on an incident in the Cervantes classic. Later a slightly different version was presented in St. Petersburg. In 1877 the mammoth and cumbersome four-act ballet *La Bayadère* received its premiere. Mostly known now for its magnificent final act, "The Kingdom of the Shades," the ballet has choreography of great beauty throughout. The ballerina Ekaterina Vazem, who created roles in eight of Petipa's ballets, danced the leading role. Though a fine technician, she was sometimes criticized for her lack of dramatic ability and her somewhat aloof stage presence.

In 1881 what Petipa referred to as "a superb blossoming of all the arts" began with the appointment of the new director of the Imperial theatres, Ivan S. Vsevolojski. It was he who was directly responsible for the change in musical direction at the Imperial theatres. Until this time composers for ballet had been lesser talents, such as Pugni and Minkus. Vsevolojski brought in Piotr Tchaikovsky, and the great composer's collaboration with Petipa must rank as one of the most significant events in the history of ballet. A former Minister of the Interior, and a man of wide and cultured tastes, Vsevolojski knew that what was required of Petipa by the court circles, who formed a large part of the theatre audience, was escapist entertainment, glamour, and novelty. He encouraged Petipa to create along these lines and the once proud choreographer deferred to his wishes. Vsevolojski's years at the helm of the Imperial Ballet were witness to many masterpieces, among them Tchaikovsky's *The Sleeping Beauty* and *Swan Lake*, Glazunov's *Raymonda* and *Ruses d'Amour*, and Drigo's *Harlequinade*.

Petipa's own creative years in Russia produced forty-three ballets. Comparatively few of these are recalled with any accuracy, but enough of his choreography remains to provide a record and a living testimony to one of the most prolific choreographers who ever lived. His best ballets contained dance after dance of sustained and inventive movement, variations and combinations, pas de deux and ensembles. His full-length roles are a goal for young ballerinas today, just as they were a hundred or so years ago, while his minor roles have often been for newcomers the first rungs on the ladder of success.

Petipa's ballets provided many of the children at the ballet school with their first stage experience, for he created numerous roles for fledgling dancers—pages, attendants, fairies, and so on. The lucky ones who were selected to appear in the ballets were doubly fortunate in being able to take part in rehearsals that were conducted by Petipa himself, frequently in the presence of the great Tchaikovsky. The composer loved the youngsters and endeared himself to them by handing out candy to the children taking part in the rehearsals. Until the beginning of the twentieth century two violinists customarily accompanied the dancers at rehearsals, sometimes supplemented by a pianist. Little could the young dancers have known that the soaring melodies to which they were dancing would for many years to come provide inspiration for full-scale productions throughout the world.

*W*orking alongside Petipa during the last years of the nineteenth century was a man of entirely different personality. Lev Ivanov, one of the few Russian-born ballet masters of the eighteenth and nineteenth centuries, was born in 1834. He graduated in 1852 and six years later was teaching junior classes at the theatre school. He appears to have been an efficient and kindly teacher. Ivanov's versatility as a dancer was pronounced, however, and had been noted even before his official graduation. He had appeared on the stage while still a student. The custom was that when a pupil reached the age of sixteen, he was eligible to serve professionally, even though his official graduation from school would in all likelihood be later. Ivanov was so diffident in manner that he was often overlooked by the administration of the Imperial theatres — even, it must be said, by Petipa himself, who on occasion took credit for work that was Ivanov's. Nevertheless, Ivanov left a small store of choreographic masterpieces. The world remembers him as the choreographer of the original *Nutcracker*, staged according to Petipa's original plans, and even more for the second and fourth acts of *Swan Lake*, which are preserved relatively intact. It has been suggested that Ivanov might also have been responsible for the "Vision Scene" in Petipa's production of *The Sleeping Beauty*, but this has not been proved.

Ivanov has an honored place in the history books as one of the theatre school's most distinguished graduates. His choreographic hallmarks remain his exceptional musicality, beautiful ensembles, and the poetic imagery and expressiveness of his pas de deux. While Petipa's choreography evokes the sparkle and precision of a magnificent diamond, Ivanov's more lyrical style has the glowing luster of a pearl.

*W*hile the Imperial Ballet was headed by these two remarkable ballet masters, the ballet department of the theatre school was rich in excellent teachers. Some of the finest in its history were now in charge, among them Christian Johansson, who began to teach at the school in 1860. In 1869 he was appointed a principal teacher. As a dancer, Johansson was known for his fabulous jumps and elegant appearance. These academic virtues could be traced to his Franco-Danish training in Copenhagen (under the direction of August Bournonville), and Johansson could boast a ballet pedigree going back to Vestris. He was responsible for giving the Russian school the pure and refined style for which the French school was famous, and he used to tell his pupils, "The Russian school is the French school, only the French have forgotten it." To this his pupil Nikolai Legat would add that not only had the Russians preserved the French school, but they had poured into it their Russian soul. And indeed the distinctiveness of Russian dance does come as much from the Russian character (what Pushkin called "its soul-inspired flight") as from its Italian and French heritage.

Johansson taught at the theatre school for more than thirty years, until just a few weeks before his death, in 1903. In his final years he taught while seated in a chair, accompanying himself on the fiddle. When giving a dancer a correction, he would summon her forward by peremptorily pointing his fiddle in her direction. Johansson was famous for his wonderful enchaînements, richly invented, never repeated. The great ballerina Tamara Karsavina called them "a wonder of modulation and diversity—a coloratura of the dance."

Johansson's classes were a source of inspiration not only to his pupils but also to Petipa, who used to drop by when in need of ideas for male choreography. This was an area in which Petipa was weak. Male dancing, so long pushed into the background, had only returned to prominence in the final years of the nineteenth century, and the new techniques had to be accommodated. Johansson would wink and say, "The old un's pinched some more!"

The virtues of the Franco-Danish school that Johansson taught to his pupils were lightness of jump, precise beats, and brilliant turns. Those pupils included his daughter Anna, Pavel Gerdt, and the brothers Nikolai and Sergei Legat. All but the last (who died young in tragic circumstances) became teachers following Johansson's traditions. Among his pupils during the last years of the nineteenth century were Olga Preobrajenskaya, Matilda Kschessinskaya, Tamara Karsavina, and Anna Pavlova, who would in a few years astound the world with their artistry. Johansson's years must be regarded as a golden age for Russian ballet.

*I*n 1885 St. Petersburg was amazed by the arrival of a new dance personality. This was the Italian ballerina Virginia Zucchi. Then thirty-eight years old, "the divine Virginia" made her debut not with the Imperial Ballet but with an Italian variety troupe at the Krassnosselski Theatre. The revue in which Zucchi appeared was entitled *Away with Sadness*, and though it does not seem to have been anything special, Zucchi herself caused a sensation. St. Petersburg balletomanes flocked to see this wonderful creature who displayed such flamboyance, dramatic sensuality, and unusual technique. Never before had Russian audiences seen such breathtaking speed, such strong point work, or, for that matter, such brief tutus! The director of the Imperial theatres, urged on by the court, lost no time in presenting Zucchi with a contract to dance with the Imperial Ballet.

Two years later, in the summer of 1887, more Italians arrived, and the excitement was renewed. This time Enrico Cecchetti caused most of the furor. With his brother and the ballerina Giovanna Limido, he had arrived to perform with an Italian ballet group at the Arcadia, a summer entertainment center. The performances were attended by all the dancers of the Imperial Theatre, as well as Petipa himself, and the director, Vsevolojski. It was said that Cecchetti's brilliant pirouettes resembled a cyclone. In every respect he was a virtuoso such as St. Petersburg had not seen for decades. The same year also marked the debut in St. Petersburg of Carlotta Brianza, a twenty-year-old ballerina of amazing skill. Both Cecchetti and Brianza were given Imperial Theatre contracts.

The Italian dance invasion continued, and in 1893 Pierina Legnani astounded everyone by executing thirty-two fouettés during a perfor-

Pierina Legnani and Sergei Legat

mance of Petipa's *Cinderella* at the Maryinsky Theatre. Russian audiences had never seen this spectacular feat before, which was repeated at a later performance in the third act of *Swan Lake*. From then on, fouettés were there to stay. Soon Russian dancers, headed by the magnificent Matilda Kschessinskaya (one-time mistress of the then Tsarevich, later Nicholas II) were able to master the new Italian technique. They learned how "to spot" during turns, how to balance with breathtaking aplomb, how to run on point, and other spectacular fireworks that had at one time awed them so.

Kschessinskaya described in her *Memoirs* the impact Zucchi had on her as an impressionable fourteen-year-old: "From the day that Zucchi appeared on our stage I began to work with fire, energy and application; my one dream was to emulate her." Mikhail Fokine was another young pupil of the theatre school who remembered the excitement of those days. He recounted in his biography how as a thirteen-year-old he witnessed Legnani for the first time spinning around in her thirty-two fouettés, without moving an inch from the spot. Fokine, who was taking the role of a page boy in the ballet *Cinderella,* began to applaud furiously, quite forgetting that he was part of the action. For this unprofessional behavior the youngster was soundly berated.

If Petipa was crushed by the evidence of the Italians' superior technical strength, he did not show it, but went on to create many of the ballets that are now justly regarded as among his very best. *The Sleeping Beauty* was first given in 1890, and Carlotta Brianza was cast (at the wish of the authorities) rather than Marie Petipa in the leading role of Princess Aurora. Her partner was Pavel Gerdt, a good-looking, graceful dancer of impeccable stage manner, who was adored by the public. Early on in his career an injury to his knee had made him diffident of virtuosity, but as a partner he was without peer. Petipa wanted Cecchetti to play the fairy Carabosse and Cecchetti agreed, but only if he were also given the role of the Blue Bird. Petipa relented and Cecchetti choreographed the part for himself so that it showed not only his exceptional virtuosity but also his imaginative ability as a mime. His partner, the Princess Florisse, was danced by the statuesque Varvara Nikitina, while the Lilac Fairy, a mime role, was undertaken by Petipa's daughter Marie.

That year Cecchetti became an assistant ballet master at the Imperial Ballet, and two years later, in 1892, he was appointed to a teaching position at the theatre school. Thus the senior girls were fortunate in having both Cecchetti (the Italian school) and Gerdt (the Franco-Russian school) as teachers, while the senior boys' class was given by Johansson's favorite pupil, Nikolai Legat. Johansson continued to hold his Class of Perfection. The dancers thrived under such leadership. Cecchetti, a pupil of Giovanni Lepri, who was in turn a pupil of the great theoretician of ballet Carlo Blasis, was as famed for his meticulous methods as Johansson and Didelot before him. In contrast to Johansson, who never repeated a combination in class, Cecchetti gave identical classes, one for each separate day of the week.

Matilda Kschessinskaya with her father

And so it was that the Russian dance in St. Petersburg developed. The British critic and historian Arnold Haskell sums it up with insight and a dash of poetry in a booklet, *Russian Ballet and the Russian School:*

Russian dancing is an arrow shot into the air, the parabola thrown by the fountains of Peterhof. It is total dancing, the complete expressiveness of the body. It is thought and emotion, will and instinct. It is the break through the technical barrier. It is simplicity in the grand manner. It is Pavlova's final flutter as the Dying Swan, her flirtatious gaiety with a fan. It is Karsavina, the girl, awakening, a woman after her rose-drenched dream. It is the spirit and the noble carriage of Semeonova. It is Ulanova-Giselle transforming a sentimental anecdote into a deathless story of love.

It is a dialogue between Petipa and Vaganova, whose busts face each other across the rehearsal rooms in Rossi Street. They speak from St. Petersburg to Leningrad.

The twentieth century brought with it many changes. The beginning of the end of Petipa was probably Vsevolojski's resignation in 1899 to become director of the Hermitage Museum. The newly appointed Prince Sergei Wolkonsky might well have been Petipa's ally had he remained in the position, but a misunderstanding with the prima ballerina assoluta Matilda Kschessinskaya hastened his resignation in 1902, and Wolkonsky's ambitious successor was an ex-cavalry officer, Colonel Vladimir Teliakovsky. Teliakovsky, who had made a serious study of music in his youth, swiftly set about reforming the Imperial Ballet and removing Petipa from his active position as ballet-master-in-chief. The ultimate humiliation for Petipa came in 1903 with the premiere of *The Magic Mirror*, which was to be his final ballet. A hostile demonstration thought to have been engineered by Teliakovsky himself greeted the work. The Imperial family, who were attending the performance, witnessed the sad scene, and Petipa was retired by the authorities shortly after. It did not soften the blow that he retained his salary, for he was barred from the theatre that he had served faithfully for sixty years. Bitter and disillusioned, Petipa died on July 1, 1910. It was the end of an era.

Some years before Petipa's death, however, the face of the Imperial Ballet had begun to change. With the introduction of the Italian technique to the Imperial School, both the dancers and the dancing began to look different. A new generation was making its presence felt.

Tsarist splendor was at its height in these last doomed years, and the exquisite Maryinsky Theatre was the perfect setting for a glittering bejeweled audience. Named for the Empress Marie, the theatre, built in 1860, became the home of the Imperial Ballet in 1889. Inside the white, gold, and turquoise-blue auditorium, five tiers of seats, huge crystal chandeliers, and tiny twinkling lights were part of the opulence. Facing the stage in the middle of the first tier was the vast Royal Box (today it seats leading dignitaries) with its heavy blue draperies and gilded surroundings. The magnificence of the scene when officers bedecked with decorations and their richly gowned ladies promenaded through the foyers rivaled the fantasies onstage.

Among the St. Petersburg dancers adored by the knowledgeable but cliquey balletomanes of the time were the great Matilda Kschessinskaya, Anna Pavlova, Vera Trefilova, and Olga Preobrajenskaya. But it was not a notable epoch only for danseuses: these years also produced a few amazing young men, among them the brothers Nikolai and Sergei Legat and particularly Mikhail Fokine.

Pavlova's wish to enter the Imperial Ballet School had been with her since the age of eight, when she went to the Maryinsky to see *The Sleeping Beauty*. Her mind was immediately made up. She would be a dancer. "I laid siege to my mother's resistance and vanquished it," she wrote. Two years later, at the age of ten, the frail dark-eyed child was one of eight accepted into the Imperial School. Pavlova likened the school to a convent, "whence frivolity is banned and where merciless discipline reigns." Only six years later she began the career that was soon to take her all over the world. She became the idol and inspiration of millions, the most beloved ballerina the world has ever known. "A dazzling meteor," the great critic Valerian Svetlov called her, and J. L. Vandoyer wrote, "Pavlova means to the dance what a Racine is to poetry, a Poussin to painting, a Gluck to music."

Yelena Lucom

The early years of the twentieth century saw the dawn of a new period in Russian ballet. A revolutionary spirit was sweeping the land and the dancers of the Imperial Ballet, as well as the older students at the theatre school, were caught up in this wind of change. Sheltered though they were, it was impossible for these curious young people to remain ignorant of the country's turmoil. Rumblings of discontent, strikes, and uprisings were increasing. The majority of Russians were still impoverished and uneducated, but the new, enlightened middle class in the cities was determined to overthrow a Tsarist regime it considered an obstacle to Russian progress. The impressions of one of the first ballerinas of the Soviet ballet, Yelena Lucom, were quoted in Natalia Roslavleva's book, *Era of the Russian Ballet:*

Winter of 1905. I was a child then, but I remember endless talk about strikes and risings that were quite incomprehensible for me. There was a general mood of disquiet. Lessons were over in haste. Lights were hardly put on at the school and we were strictly forbidden to approach the thickly curtained windows. We wandered through the school building, peering into the faces of the grown-ups, hoping to detect and understand what was being hidden from us.

Lucom remembers that at the end of one performance the children were

pushed into the coach, that rushed at an unprecedented pace through the dark streets. I remember to this day the whistles, the rattle of carts loaded with something, and the shouts of the crowd. All that night, almost until the break of dawn, we tried, with our little childish minds, to penetrate beyond the mystery of political events that were so carefully concealed from us by officials.

Influenced by the momentous events outside their artistic confines, the employed dancers of the Tsar, led by Pavlova, Karsavina, and Fokine, soon petitioned for improved artistic conditions. Their attempts to gain certain meager concessions came to nothing. Sergei Legat, a deeply involved member of the dancers' committee who was forced to retreat from his beliefs, committed suicide as a result.

Teliakovsky, the régisseur Nikolai Sergueeff, and other members of the administration had blocked the artists' demands, but they by no means crushed the spirit of the leaders of the dancers' revolt. Fokine continued to be a vigorous opponent of the bureaucratic management of the ballet, and his outspoken opposition to many administration policies soon brought him into disfavor.

Fokine, however, was too talented to be ignored. The rising male star of the Imperial Ballet, he had since his graduation in 1898 appeared as the Prince and the Blue Bird in *The Sleeping Beauty*, as Colin in *La Fille Mal Gardée*, the Prince in *The Nutcracker*, and Basil in *Don Quixote*. From 1902 he had been teaching the senior girls at the school. His ambition led him to choreography. Attracted to Longus's story *Daphnis and Chloë*, Fokine in 1904 prepared a scenario for a ballet in two acts. Accompanying this scenario was a memorandum to the theatre administration that laid out with the most precise logic Fokine's ideas for the reform of ballet and his visions for its future. The ballet was turned down and the memorandum rejected. Later in his life Fokine recounted how he had been proclaimed a "heretic" for these artistic beliefs. The following year, however, he was given the opportunity to stage a revival of *Acis et Galatea*, mounted by his students. Galatea was played by the eighteen-year-old Maria Gorshakova, who recalled in her memoirs how the gifted young choreographer demanded absolute accuracy of style. Before the rehearsal period he assembled the dancers and explained in depth his intentions and "what each of us had to represent." Also in this production was Vaslav Nijinsky, still a few years away from his graduation, but already beginning to be noticed for his strength and soaring jumps.

Fokine's father had agreed only with reluctance that his son should enter the theatre school ("I do not want my Mimotchka to become a jumping jack"), but Fokine went on to become one of the most remarkable choreographers of the century, a true innovator who set ballet on a new path. Among his ballets still performed today are *Chopiniana* (known in the West as *Les Sylphides*), *Carnaval*, *Schéhérazade*, *Le Spectre de la Rose*, *Prince Igor*, and *Petrushka*.

Soon after Fokine's first venture into choreography, Isadora Duncan visited Russia. Her impact was enormous, and her influence continues to be felt in that country. In her biography, *My Art*, Duncan calls herself

Mikhail Fokine in *Daphnis and Chloë*

"an enemy of ballet," and goes on to describe a visit that she made to the theatre school in St. Petersburg in 1905:

I . . . arose at the unheard of hour of eight o'clock to visit the Imperial Ballet School, where I saw all the little pupils standing in rows, and going through those torturous exercises. They stood on the tips of their toes for hours, like so many victims of a cruel and unnecessary Inquisition. The great, bare dancing rooms, devoid of any beauty or inspiration, with a large picture of the Tsar as the only relief on the walls, were like a torture-chamber. I was more than ever convinced that the Imperial Ballet School is an enemy to nature and art.

Though Duncan railed against ballet as an artificial discipline, many in the ballet world were fired with enthusiasm by the possibilities she opened up with her freedom of gesture and her sense of plastique. Among those who gloried in her art were Fokine and the Moscow choreographer, who was trained in St. Petersburg, Alexander Gorsky.

A few years earlier, in 1902, a young dancer had graduated from the theatre school. Like Pavlova she became a legend in her time. But unlike Pavlova she lived a full life, teaching and coaching generations of English ballet dancers. She died in 1978, at the age of ninety-three. Tamara Karsavina, like all graduates of the period, went through the obligatory examination before the theatre authorities. After receiving the highest marks possible, she was accepted into the company, as everyone knew she would be. While still a schoolgirl studying under her father, Platon Karsavin, and Pavel Gerdt, she had been picked out for her enormous potential and expressiveness. A few years later she was being praised for her great lyricism, sense of poetry, and feeling for music.

Six years after Karsavina's graduation, a young man named Vaslav Nijinsky entered the company. In her autobiography Karsavina tells how when she first saw him in class, leaping "high above the heads of the others" and then seeming to hover in the air, she asked, "Who is this?" of the teacher Mikhail Obukhov. "It is Nijinsky; the little devil never comes down with the music," was the reply. It amazed Karsavina that word had not yet got out of this prodigious talent, so soon to graduate from the school. Obukhov laughed and told her that soon it would. How right he was, for within a few brief years, in partnership with Karsavina, Nijinsky was known throughout the West as the most exceptional male dancer the world had ever seen, famed not just for his jumps but for his uncanny ability to transform a part into something so personal that it became unforgettable. With Karsavina, he went on to create a whole galaxy of roles, many of them in Fokine's ballets—the Poet in *Les Sylphides*, *Petrushka*, the Harlequin in *Carnaval*, *Spectre de la Rose*. He choreographed four hauntingly different ballets for himself: *Jeux*, *L'Après-midi d'un Faune*, *Le Sacre du Printemps*, and *Tyl Eulenspiegel*. Soon after Nijinsky's graduation he joined the Diaghilev company and took leaves of absence from the Imperial Theatre (with Karsavina, Fokine, and other artists of the Imperial Ballet who had been assembled to tour Europe).

Anna Pavlova

Павлова II.

38

Nijinsky's fame increased until 1918, when he had a mental breakdown. He never recovered, and died in London in 1950 .

_S_ergei Diaghilev, the impresario of the Ballet Russe, had worked with Prince Wolkonsky in an official capacity at the Imperial Theatre. Brought up in Perm, Diaghilev moved to St. Petersburg in 1890 to study law. Gifted and brilliant, he soon found himself at the center of the cultural activities of the city. As an outlet for his artistic interests Diaghilev founded in 1899 a magazine called *The World of Art* (in Russian, *Mir Iskustva*) in association with a group of artists, stage designers, and musicians, among them Leon Bakst and Alexander Benois. After the discontinuation of the magazine in 1904 Diaghilev was responsible for the presentation of art exhibitions in Europe and Russia.

His first venture as an impresario occurred in 1908 with the presentation of Feodor Chaliapin in *Boris Godunov* in Paris. A year later Paris was to witness one of the most successful and triumphant seasons in the history of ballet when Diaghilev brought over a group of dancers from the Imperial Theatre, including Pavlova, Karsavina, Fokine, Nijinsky, Adolfe Bolm, and Mikhail Mordkin (from the Moscow Ballet). The repertory was composed of works by Fokine, and the choreographer's reputation in Europe was instantly established.

Diaghilev's seasons in Europe continued until 1927. Many of the dancers did return to the Imperial theatres to fulfill their contracts with the management, but in most cases their loyalties shifted to the West, and many of the Imperial Ballet's best dancers were lost forever to the Russian ballet. The exodus continued throughout the Revolutionary and post-Revolutionary years. Diaghilev himself remained in the West and died in Paris in 1931.

After the first company of dancers left Russia, there graduated a fresh group who were to have an enormous effect on the ballet abroad. They included George Balanchine, Alexandra Danilova, Olga Spessivtzeva, and the very young Tamara Geva. After considerable difficulty this new group succeeded in leaving for the West and met up with Diaghilev in Paris. They were invited to join his company, by now bereft of some of its earlier stars.

With his enormous taste, flair, and ability to spot genuine talent Diaghilev was undoubtedly the major influence on dance in the early part of the twentieth century. He altered the course of dance history, not only in Russia but also in Europe and America. Without Fokine, Massine, Balanchine, and the staggering constellation of talented dancers who later carried on the tradition of Russian training as teachers, ballet might never have reached the pinnacle of perfection it has today, as evidenced in America by the works of Balanchine and in England by those of Sir Frederick Ashton, who was influenced by many of the Russians but particularly by Pavlova and Bronislava Nijinska, Nijinsky's sister.

The departure to the West of many of Russia's most important dancers left a void, and had it not been for a few miraculous events, the ballet might never have recovered. The Russian Revolution of 1917 naturally affected the country's artistic institutions, many of which had been under Imperial patronage. The ballet was one of the first to suffer. Conditions following the Revolution were appalling. Everything, including culture, was in a state of turmoil. The very existence of ballet, long regarded as the plaything of kings and aristocrats, was threatened.

In Balanchine's biography we read that the fourteen-year-old ballet student had to support himself and the aunt he lived with through a variety of jobs unconnected with the theatre. In return, he was given scraps of food or some other material reward. Others were in similar straits. Theatre Street became a gathering place for displaced students. Daily they would go there in the hope of finding that the school, closed since the Revolution, had reopened.

Finally, primarily because of the efforts of the first Soviet Commissar of Education, Anatole Lunacharsky, the school opened once again. Performances at the Maryinsky were initially given free to the general public. Gradually order and normality returned. The Maryinsky was renamed the Kirov Theatre, and the ballet school became the State Choreographic Institute.

Many ballerinas from the Imperial Ballet returned to take part in reviving the Soviet ballet, including Elizaveta Gerdt, daughter of Pavel Gerdt. In the first years after the Revolution an organization known as the "Proletkult" took charge of culture throughout the land. Concerned above all with founding a new art for a revolutionary society, it insisted that scenarios be changed to appeal to the new audiences. Petipa's *King Candaules*, for instance, was given a new story line: the heroine became a shepherd girl who leads a rebellion against the king. Proletkult lasted only until 1922. After its demise genuine experiment based on tradition began to flower. Feodor Lopukhov invented a new plastique form of choreography, possibly influenced by Fokine's earlier innovations but very much his own, and in Moscow Kasyan Goleizovsky delved into a fresh style of movement. Both these choreographers are said to have been an influence on the young Balanchine, whose first ventures into choreography occurred about this time.

Despite Lopukhov's avant-garde leanings, he was immensely knowledgeable about classical ballet. In 1922 Petipa's *The Sleeping Beauty* was revived under his supervision. This new production retained the original choreography but added the now famous Lilac Fairy variation, choreographed by Lopukhov himself. Certain other changes appropriate to the times were made. Elizaveta Gerdt danced the opening performance, and Olga Spessivtzeva was one of the other Auroras during these first revivals.

The brilliant Spessivtzeva had graduated from the St. Petersburg Theatre School in 1913 and had been one of the ballerinas to dance in the West with the Diaghilev Ballet. She was a true romantic, pale and

Olga Spessivtzeva

40

luminously lovely. Her huge eyes, long, slim neck, and sleek dark hair brought irresistibly to mind the lithographs of Elssler. Like Taglioni, she became one of the great Giselles. Unable to endure the stresses of the world, Spessivtzeva suffered for years from mental illness. Now, thanks to newly discovered drugs, she has recovered and lives quietly in upstate New York at the Tolstoy farm near Nyack.

In the early years following the Revolution the school saw many changes. A far more diverse curriculum, including such subjects as dance history, the study and theory of music, and the rudiments of staging and set design, was introduced. It was a time of self-sacrificing hard work on the part of teachers and students alike, but also a rewarding period of exploration and discovery. These years produced scores of dancers and choreographers who worked to restore Russian ballet following the ordeals of the recent past.

Elizaveta Gerdt

*I*n addition to the beautiful and elegant Elizaveta Gerdt, there was Yelena Lucom, who had graduated in 1909. She was one of the few ballerinas to return to Russia and remain there after performing with Diaghilev in the West. Her artistic training had been with the old Maryinsky, but she acquired from the Soviet school a freer, more athletic approach, the use of big lifts, and emotional expressiveness.

Other important dancers of the period were the premier danseur Konstantin Sergeyev, Piotr Gusev, and the great dramatic dancer Vakhtang Chabukiani. In addition, there was the splendid and versatile Alexei Yermolayev. The lyrical ballerinas Marina Semeonova and Galina Ulanova graduated in 1925 and became the great ballerinas of the thirties and forties. Ulanova and Semeonova's teacher was Agrippina Vaganova, who had joined the Maryinsky Ballet in 1897. A dancer of much technical strength, often referred to as the "Queen of Variations," she was not named a ballerina until 1915. Soon afterward Vaganova retired from dancing, having completed her obligatory twenty years. In 1921 she returned to the State Choreographic Institute to devote herself to the formation of the new Soviet school of ballet.

Vaganova, who later gave her name to the school, had an influence that cannot be overestimated. Plain of feature, with a somewhat thick-set physique, she was an inspired teacher. A pupil of Ivanov, Pavel Gerdt, Ekaterina Vazem, and Nikolai Legat, Vaganova had also learned much from watching the classes of Cecchetti. From all these influences she created a system of teaching that soon had her pupils dancing in a new and distinctive way. More expansive, more eloquent, with emphasis on the correct position of the spine, making for a strong yet pliant back, the Vaganova method produced dancers capable of great elevation. Nora Kovach, the Hungarian ballerina who defected to the West in the 1950s, was one of Vaganova's favorite pupils, among the privileged few who received private coaching. She recalls how Vaganova would work endlessly on the tiniest detail. Ports de bras were extremely important to her, as well as details such as the use of the hands, the head, and the eyes. Changing any of these, however minutely, resulted in different meanings, different inflections. Says Kovach, "I do remember also how important she considered the 'soul' of a dancer, for this is what she felt made one dancer different from another."

Another of her pupils, the well-known New York teacher (originally from Rumania) Gabriella Taub-Darvash, talked to me of Vaganova's emphasis on coordination, how she insisted that the arms finish the movement of the legs. She demanded that the sharpness of the footwork, the ending, not show in the arms and in the hands, nor the ports de bras reveal whatever technical problems the dancer might be having with the legs. In a jump or, say, a glissade assemblé, Vaganova wanted the arms to continue moving upward after the feet finished, to make the enchaînement look twice as expressive, to give the audience the illusion that the dancer was still in the air after she had landed on the stage.

Yuri Grigorovich, artistic director of the Bolshoi Ballet, in a recent conversation recalled his impressions of Vaganova. Never a pupil of hers, he sometimes watched her classes from the upper balcony of the main rehearsal room. "Her very presence would electrify the students," he said. "She had great authority. If she liked you, she could be wonderful. Always her corrections were absolutely to the point and specific. She had a terrific eye for showing the precise form and style."

Vaganova's vocabulary was rich, and she had many little tricks to help the dancer look her best. She demonstrated the steps she taught, and the effect was amazing. Vaganova's scientific methods of teaching are responsible for the distinctive style of the Soviet school of dancing.

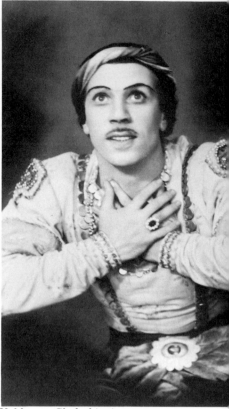

Vakhtang Chabukiani

At one time the St. Petersburg (Leningrad) and Moscow schools were quite dissimilar, the former being more refined, the latter more flamboyant, more dramatic. To an extent these differences still exist, but nowadays the two schools are far closer in style. Many of the Leningrad dancers, including Semeonova, Gerdt, and Ulanova, moved early in their careers to Moscow. Currently they are molding the new generation of Moscow dancers, and among Gerdt's pupils have been such dancers as Maya Plisetskaya, Raissa Struchkova, and Ekaterina Maximova.

In 1934 Vaganova's textbook on ballet, *Fundamentals of the Classic Dance,* was published, and three years later it appeared in an English translation by Anatole Chujoy.

Vaganova taught at the State Choreographic Institute until her death, in 1951. Her pupils, in addition to those already mentioned, include several generations of dancers who have left their mark on Soviet ballet and even that of the West. Some of the best known are Vera Volkova, Olga Jordan, Fea Balabina, Natalia Dudinskaya, Alla Shelest, Alla Ossipenko, and Irina Kolpakova.

Valery Panov was one of the male pupils selected by her for special coaching. Though Vaganova's methods were constant, she recognized the individuality of each of her pupils, and she encouraged self-criticism in all of them. A perfectionist herself, she insisted upon perfection in others.

Panov graduated from the Kirov with the highest marks of the year. Two decades later he was to say of Vaganova: "Her coaching was directly responsible for my growth as a dancer. After studying with her, I understood what type of artist I was. There was just one way for me." Panov, who began his career with the Maly, was transferred to the Kirov as a principal dancer soon after Nureyev's defection; many leading roles were created for him during his years with the company.

_I_n the decades following the Revolution Soviet ballet discovered itself. New choreographers came to the fore, including Leonid Lavrovsky, Leonid Jacobson, Rotislav Zakharov, and Vassily Vainonen. Among the most popular ballets of the period, most of them politically oriented, were _The Red Poppy, Katerina, the Serf Ballerina, The Flames of Paris_ (set during the French Revolution), _The Fountains of Bakhchisarai_ (in which Ulanova found one of her greatest roles), and _Laurencia_.

Classical ballets continued to be seen alongside the new Soviet realism. _Giselle, Esmeralda, The Little Hump-backed Horse, Don Quixote, The Sleeping Beauty, Swan Lake_, and _Raymonda_ reached vast new audiences and proved afresh their popularity.

Only a year or so before the siege of Leningrad crippled the city for two ghastly years (1941–1943), one of the greatest of all Soviet ballets was produced. This was Leonid Lavrovsky's _Romeo and Juliet_, which was choreographed to an original score by Sergei Prokofiev. The leading roles were danced by Galina Ulanova and Konstantin Sergeyev. _Romeo and Juliet_ fulfilled all of Fokine's prophecies and dreams for a new Russian style of ballet. Music, drama, and dancing here united to form a perfect whole. The ensembles were genuinely integrated into the action of the story, and each individual had his own part to play. Shakespeare's Verona came to life. In 1956 the ballet, performed by Moscow's Bolshoi Ballet, was seen for the first time in London, revealing to sophisticated balletomanes a whole new concept of ballet making— massive, almost operatic in structure, and above all expressive.

Five years later it was the Kirov Ballet's turn to make its first major visit to the West. The company appeared in both Paris and London. For many in Europe it was their first view of the school of dancing that had derived, via Vaganova, from the great Imperial School. Vaganova's last pupil, Irina Kolpakova, and the prima ballerinas Inna Zubkovskaya, Alla Sizova, Natalia Makarova, and Alla Ossipenko all enjoyed well-justified triumphs, as did the premier danseurs Vladilen Semenov, Yuri Soloviev, Sergei Vikulov, and the character dancer Anatole Gridin.

The season introduced the work of the imaginative young choreographer Yuri Grigorovich. Trained at the school by Boris Shavrov, Alexei Pisarev, Vladimir Ponamarov, Alexander Pushkin, and André Lopukhov (brother of Feodor), Grigorovich graduated in 1946 as a demi-caractère dancer, but from the beginning he showed an aptitude for choreography, and had even tried his hand at it while still a student. His ballet _The_

Stone Flower had been his first major success. He went on to create another, *The Legend of Love*. His acclaim made him the inevitable choice to replace Leonid Lavrovsky, after his death, in 1964, as director of the Bolshoi, a post he still holds.

Since its first visit to Europe in 1961, the Kirov Ballet has been confronted with various setbacks, among them the loss of some of its best dancers to the West. The first to go was the brilliant Rudolf Nureyev.

Nureyev, the dancer whose name is now known throughout the world, was born in 1938 in a train traveling through Siberia. An only son, he still remembers vividly the poverty of his childhood in Uffa. From his earliest years his deep love of music sustained him, and soon the discovery of the joys of dancing led to the desire to take up ballet. When he finally reached Leningrad at the age of seventeen, after years of local study, he was informed: "You'll either be a brilliant dancer or a total failure." Nureyev's determination and innate genius, together with the inspired teaching of Alexander Pushkin, saw to it that the former came true.

At the school Nureyev led a lonely life without any real friends. According to Alexander Minz, his contemporary, "He seemed like some kind of fanatic. People just did not know what to make of him." A compulsive worker, he would prepare solos all by himself for hours on end in an empty studio after the others had left. "I would invite Pushkin to come and demand of him if I was doing it right or wrong," said Nureyev. Under Pushkin's guidance, Nureyev made phenomenal progress. "At first it seemed as if the Kirov did not want me. Boris Shavrov—a senior teacher—was determined that I should go back to Uffa. After a competition in Moscow, the Bolshoi came and asked me to be a soloist. Stanislavsky also wanted me as a principal dancer. I told them that I was just finishing school because, really, I wanted to join the Kirov. I had not yet been notified if they were taking me, but Pushkin told me not to worry, to wait till the graduation performance. The performance went extremely, extremely well. One matinee when I was dancing *Diana and Acteon*, Dudinskaya met me on the staircase and said, 'What is this I hear, that you are going to Moscow? Stay here and dance with me.' So that's how it was. I danced with her *Laurencia*, *Gayane*, *Corsaire*, and *Diana and Acteon*, and in the winter I danced *Swan Lake* and *Giselle*. Basically all my repertory was prepared in school, and in the official year when I was supposed to finish I did *Nutcracker*."

Alexander Minz told me that when Dudinskaya asked Nureyev to dance with her while still a student it caused a sensation. Nureyev remembers the rave review in *Pravda* following the performance. Such a thing was practically unprecedented in a paper that had no regular ballet critic on its staff.

The story of his defection at the airport in Paris just before the London season in 1961 is well known. One of the Kirov's loveliest and most graceful ballerinas, Natalia Makarova, remained behind during the company's third visit to London in 1970. Alexander Minz, a valued character soloist, left as an émigré in 1972. Mikhail Baryshnikov, the extraordinarily talented golden boy of the Kirov, winner of the 1968 Varna Gold Medal and the first-prize winner at the Moscow Competition of 1972, elected to remain in Canada during a tour in the summer of 1974.

Baryshnikov had auditioned for the Kirov at the age of fifteen during a visit to Leningrad from his hometown, Riga. Alexander Pushkin's reputation as a teacher prompted Baryshnikov to approach him and ask if he could be one of his pupils. According to Baryshnikov, Pushkin examined him "like a horse," and asked him to jump up and down. He was then quickly escorted to the school's doctors, who examined him further. Then came months of waiting. "Seeing Leningrad and the school was like an electric shock. I could not imagine living away from it," he told me. Once he was with the school, Baryshnikov discovered that Pushkin's teaching was all he had dreamed it would be. "He taught the most logical series of steps and movements that I had ever seen. He knew the classical dance completely." As for Leningrad, it was "the most beautiful city in the world, my city." Now living in the West, Baryshnikov describes himself as having "a divided soul."

The same year that Baryshnikov defected, the great heroic and demi-caractère dancer Valery Panov and his young ballerina wife, Galina, finally left for Israel, after a long struggle for permission from Soviet authorities. A couple of years later the ballerina Kaleria Fedicheva emigrated to join her American husband. All these dancers needed the greater choices the West provided—freedom to dance more often, to select their companies, their choreographers.

Early in 1977 the Kirov Ballet endured another blow. Yuri Soloviev, the brilliant and much-loved virtuoso, was found dead of a self-inflicted bullet wound. Now the company, under the direction of Oleg Vinogradov, is rebuilding itself, restoring its self-respect, and looking to the West for inspiration. Roland Petit, the French choreographer, has recently choreographed *The Hunchback of Notre-Dame* for them, and overtures have been made to other Western choreographers. And there is always the school that has nurtured the company from the beginning with magnificent talents. Perhaps the next Nijinsky is waiting in the wings.

Konstantin Sergeyev   Natalia Dudinskaya   Nadezhda Federova   Yuri Oumrikhin   Angelina Armeiskaya   Alec Timoush

2.

The Children of Theatre Street Today

Lena Voronzova

Lubomir Kafka

Michaela Cerna

Whenever Agrippina Vaganova was asked why the ballet took root in Leningrad, she would reply, according to Yuri Grigorovich, that there was nothing strange about it. The city, with its graceful buildings, its well laid out streets, its splendidly designed parks and gardens, made such an achievement inevitable. The architecture of the city, like the Kirov Ballet, has beauty, harmony, and an authentic classicism. Grigorovich agrees with Vaganova that the aesthetic appeal of Leningrad has always been a potent influence on the ballet, and this same point is made many times in conversation by dancers and teachers from the Kirov. They contrast their city with Moscow, for hundreds of years a bustling center of trade, altogether more Russian, more robust, than the refined, elegant city built by Peter the Great.

For years there was rivalry as well as a distinct stylistic difference between the ballet companies of these two great but dissimilar cultural centers. When Tamara Geva (George Balanchine's first wife) auditioned for the Choreographic Academy in Moscow in 1921, the examining committee wrote on her rejection slip, "Definitely talented, but the style strictly that of Petrograd [the Russian form of St. Petersburg, by which the city was known from Russia's entry into World War I, in 1914, until Lenin's death, in 1924, when the city became Leningrad], therefore not compatible with the Bolshoi." Moscow-trained dancers were for years considered more flamboyant, more expressive, than those trained in St. Petersburg, where the style was rooted in a tradition that emphasized pure classicism.

The two companies are today much closer in manner of dancing. After the Revolution, Moscow once again became Russia's capital city, as it was in the days before Peter. As a consequence the Bolshoi, earlier regarded as the provincial branch of the Imperial Ballet, is now the more prestigious company. Today it is Leningrad that frequently loses its best talent to the Moscow company. Many of its most notable ballerinas, premiers danseurs, and ballet masters have been transferred to the Bolshoi, the latest being the brilliant Ludmilla Semenyaka. While still a pupil she was regarded as one of the great hopes of the Kirov Ballet. Since 1972 her impeccable Kirov style has graced all the classic roles at the mighty Bolshoi Theatre, as well as many of Grigorovich's modern creations.

Of course there are no shortcuts in obtaining the technical perfection acquired in the schools of either city. Nearly two hundred and fifty years of work have gone into the Vaganova Choreographic Institute's special combination of ingredients. A heaping of hard work, talent, and patient training go into the making of a Kirov dancer.

$\mathcal{A}$nyone can apply to the Vaganova Choreographic Institute, but many of the applicants are "discovered" by special talent scouts at the Pioneer Palaces (where children pursue hobbies and cultural activites) or at schools. Others are recommended by private teachers. The selection methods search out the best possible talent throughout the country. Some of the children have never had a dance lesson in their lives. The response is invariably overwhelming, for the school is justly famous, not only in Leningrad but throughout the Soviet Union.

Every spring notices are posted outside the school building on Rossi Street, notifying the general public when the entrance examinations for the coming year will take place. The location is always within the school itself. Most of the boys and girls auditioning for places are native Leningraders; others arrive from far-off towns and territories. Many are ultimately accepted by special arrangement with their governments from countries abroad, such as Hungary, Rumania, and Czechoslovakia. Occasionally students are accepted from Western countries.

A glance into any of the classrooms reveals a diversity of ethnic origins. Little girls with blond hair and high cheekbones sit side by side with small boys of Asiatic origin. Tartars, Georgians, Slavs, Mongolians, alike only in their physical beauty and neat school uniforms, sweat and toil for the same goals.

Of the thousand or so applicants each year, less than a hundred are accepted after the very demanding examination, which takes several days. The children arrive at the school, some nervous, some excited, all anticipating the moment. They are aged between eight and eleven. All are accompanied by an adult—a parent, a grandmother, or a teacher. The importance of the occasion can be detected by a look into the eyes of the older generation. Will their child be accepted? Acceptance can be the first rung on the ladder to a privileged life, and a status that the ordinary Russian cannot hope to achieve. Dancers are among the Soviet Union's most admired and envied citizens, and early on the youngsters who are chosen are reminded of their future obligations to the motherland. Before they travel abroad they are made aware that they represent the Soviet Union and must regard themselves always as special diplomats for their country. Unlike most Russians, successful dancers often have the opportunity to travel abroad. In addition, they may acquire dachas in the country as well as spacious apartments in the city.

Once the students are entered into the school, all fees are paid by the state. The costs covered include academic tuition, medical bills, holidays in the country during school vacations, and incidental needs such as uniforms and ballet shoes.

The teachers, administration officials, and doctors who make up the qualified selection team know precisely what they are searching for, and only the ideal physique can be accommodated. The hopefuls are brought in, fifteen or twenty at a time. They wait their turn, huddled shyly together on benches. When the individual is called, his or her outer garments are removed so that every bone, every muscle, is exposed to the penetrating gaze of the specialists. The right proportions of torso and limbs as well as facial features are essential, for dancers must have better-than-average looks in a performing art where their bodies are their instruments.

The child is tested for a flexible instep, a natural extension of the leg when raised in second position, and a demi-plié showing the potential for a good jump. The suppleness of the spine is also very important, and to test the flexibility of the back, the teacher bends the child backward from the waist. The toes are also looked at to see whether there might be, for instance, an unusually long second toe. This would rule out the possibility of a girl's dancing on point.

In addition to these basic physical requirements, the doctors inquire about the health of each would-be dancer. All applicants are given a thorough medical examination to test, among other things, their lungs, which must be strong. A computer, which predicts the child's future growth on the basis of his current measurements, aids the doctor in this task. After all this, another important factor is checked before a child can be admitted into the Vaganova Institute—his academic records. Dancers must be intelligent and alert in order to absorb all that is necessary during their training and later careers.

Of those who pass these rigorous examinations, only the best, the cream of the crop, are taken. Those who are turned down have the possibility of training elsewhere if they are determined enough, perhaps with the opportunity of returning for another attempt in a few years' time.

They wait their turn,
huddled shyly together on benches.
When the individual is called, his or her outer
garments are removed so that every bone,
every muscle, is exposed to the penetrating
gaze of the specialists.

The progress of the children is checked throughout their eight-year training. Each semester lasts six months, and the first few months are particularly important. If insufficient progress has been made after one year, the child is asked to leave. A child who survives the second year is generally at less risk of being replaced.

A special six-year program at the Vaganova Institute exists for talented, slightly older children. These students, who are usually twelve or thirteen years old, fill the places vacated by pupils who leave after the first year or two. Most have had some dance experience outside, perhaps with a company formed at one of the Pioneer Palaces, perhaps with a private teacher. At any rate, the newcomers must be gifted, at least up to the level of the children of comparable age in the Vaganova Institute. Natalia Makarova was one of the children accepted for the accelerated six-year course. She was thirteen years old when she entered the school. Tamara Geva was another. Both had the determination to succeed.

One of the school's most distinguished graduates, Marina Semeonova, was initially rejected. Fortunately, under the guidance of Vaganova, the decision was reversed for Semeonova, who went on to become one of the greatest of all Soviet ballerinas, famed particularly for her eloquent interpretation of Odette/Odile in *Swan Lake*. Semeonova is now a leading teacher at the Choreographic Academy in Moscow. It is her teaching that has produced many of the Bolshoi's current crop of leading dancers. Vaslav Nijinsky was another famous name nearly turned down by the examination board. Only the determined intervention of Nikolai Legat, who spotted the boy's raw potential, saved him. Nijinsky, as the world knows, became a dancer of genius.

Angelina Armeiskaya, the dark-haired, dark-eyed ten-year-old featured in the film *The Children of Theatre Street*, shows just the qualities for which the Vaganova Institute is famous. After only two years of training, this lovely long-legged youngster, with her serene gaze, already has the poise and grace of a much older dancer.

Like her, all ballet dancers, from newcomers to seasoned professionals, must begin their day with a class. In the classroom a male teacher has charge of the boys, while the girls are taught by a woman. All of them have had to master the complicated French terminology of the classroom, for ballet as an art form originated in the court of Louis XIV, and French has remained the language of ballet ever since, wherever it is performed. Holding on to the barre, the students, boys and girls alike, perform an assortment of pliés, battements tendus, and ronds de jambes, as well as fondus and frappés and much else besides, all essential to the building of the right muscles for this most demanding discipline. The exercises are always repeated on either side to give the whole body a proper workout. When the muscles are thoroughly warmed and stretched, the students move to the center of the ballet studio, where adagio exercises are performed without the aid of the barre. Positions of the feet, ports de bras, exercises for the strengthening of the back, exercises for balance, all become second nature to the children, as well as the importance of watching their line and correct placement.

By the time a girl is eleven she will in all probability be doing her first exercises on point. Within a few years she will be performing fouettés, pirouettes, and chaîne and piqué turns, all steps requiring considerable strength in the feet. The boys during this period will become proficient in the practice of multiple turns in the air and high beaten steps. Each year their elevation in jumps will become greater. The children will gradually acquire the full turnout that provides greater flexibility and range of movement, while enhancing considerably the dancers' line.

Early on in their training the young dancers will have discovered why the body must daily endure these repetitive exercises and why it is important to have a correctly positioned body. The discipline is not simply for aesthetic reasons; it is necessary to lessen the possibility of injury.

But even with all the care that is taken in training and educating a dancer, injuries do happen. A dancer learns to live with pain. It is not natural, this forcing of limbs beyond their normal limits. Nor was a girl intended to dance on the tips of her toes. Soreness and bleeding can often result; sprains and torn ligaments are also common with young as well as experienced performers. But injuries and pain are endured as an inevitable part of a dancer's life, just as they are endured by an athlete.

The school is fortunate in having on the fourth floor of its premises an infirmary that is designed to care for injuries and sicknesses of all kinds with the best equipment available. A medical staff, including a dentist and orthopedic specialists, works here full time. A masseuse is also available to soothe and ease aching limbs. Antonia Fessetchko is known by the dancers as "the comforting spirit." While she massages away the tense, cramped muscles, she listens to her patients' tales of their triumphs and despairs. Ballerinas and beginners alike have benefited from the soothing touch of her hands.

The children's diets are carefully watched over by the school staff. The meals provided in the canteen are well balanced and plentiful. Vegetable soup and salads are staples, as are meat and kasha, blinis, stews, and plenty of apples and apple juice. Like dancers everywhere, the children of Theatre Street are conscious of extra inches and watch their weight carefully.

Пластининой Ври.

Robert Dornhelm, co-director of *The Children of Theatre Street*, found himself becoming attached to the children whose lives he was documenting. His heart especially went out to those whose homes are far from Leningrad. Many of these children have been separated from their families for two years or more. "Angelina is the same age as my daughter," he told me. "Her parents live two thousand miles away and she has not been home for many months. Sometimes, seeing her so sad and lonely, I wanted to embrace her, but showing her sympathy would have made her cry."

He told me he saw a big difference between the children who
lived at home and the little community that lived in the school
dormitory just ten minutes from Theatre Street but far away from
their home towns. "With the boarders, you see little families
develop. The older girls become almost like mothers to the smaller
girls and boys. We tried to show something of this in the film in
the relationship between Lena, who was graduating that year, and
Angelina." Robert noted that the older students often help the
younger ones with their daily tasks, such as washing and ironing
clothes. All of the children are responsible for many duties around
the dormitories. They make their beds and keep their rooms tidy.

Tights and practice attire must be laundered daily, and in the canteen the older children help serve the smaller ones. Like ballet children all over the world, they become adept at caring for their own ballet shoes, learning how to sew on ribbons, darn the toes, and the like. It is a task that is never ending, for ballet slippers can be worn through at the rate of a pair a week. A professional dancer gets through them even faster. Sometimes a pair will have to be discarded by a ballerina after only one full-length ballet.

All the children who are accepted by the school, whether they come from out of town or from Leningrad itself, are required to continue their academic education. They are schooled in the classrooms of Rossi Street in a syllabus up to a secondary-school level. The Russian language and literature, foreign languages, history, geography, mathematics, and science are among the compulsory subjects. In addition, there are courses in the history of theatre, ballet, music, and art. The learning of a musical instrument is also compulsory. The school has several small music rooms where piano lessons are given. At one time the school employed Dmitri Shostakovich's sister as a teacher of music. In all of these special subjects the children are taught by the best available, all specialists in their field.

> *"Life is hard.*
> *Both my mother and my father are from families of workers.*
> *A lot of time things are hard at the school.*
> *Sometimes I want to run away from it all.*
> *But when things go well,*
> *I accept it. . . . I find the dance really hard work."*

The Rumanian dancer Sergiu Stefanschi, a former principal dancer at the National Ballet of Canada and now a teacher at the National Ballet School in Toronto, retains vivid memories of his six years spent at the school in Leningrad. He remembers with keen appreciation classes in art history given by specialists from the Hermitage Museum. "They were so informative, so knowledgeable, and their manner to us—well, they approached us knowing we were going to be artists. That meant so much to us." Sergiu recollected the teacher from Leningrad University who came in to teach literature. "She was a balletomane who would go every night to the ballet, where she had her own special seat. Because of this, she had a special interest in all of us and always had so much to say. She didn't like us to take notes: 'Please just listen; don't scribble, or you'll miss something.' "

For the children, whose lives naturally revolve around their dancing, one of the most fascinating classes is probably dance history, given by Marietta Frangopolo, curator of the museum on the fifth floor of the academy. Frangopolo was once a classmate of Balanchine's. "She was an absolute fountain of information, with a marvelous memory," says Sergiu. "She had so many stories to tell us about past generations, past traditions. Everyone loved her. She was a friend to all the children." This warm, adorable woman, who was a dancer at the Kirov Ballet for thirty years, still teaches at the school and remains one of its treasures and inspirations. The museum in her charge is filled to overflowing with mementos of the Kirov's glorious past, its years as the leading Imperial Theatre. The walls are covered from floor to ceiling with paintings and photographs of former dancers and ballet masters. Busts and statuettes adorn the shelves. Under their watchful eyes future stars immerse themselves in the immense history-laden scrapbooks where the stories of such dancers as Avdotia Istomina and the tragic Maria Danilova spring to life. Here, too, they can learn about the Soviet Union's first ballerinas who did so much to restore Russian ballet after the anguish of civil war and the economic turmoil that followed it.

It is not just in the school museum that one is conscious of the past—in fact, nowhere is it possible to escape the school's traditions. Nor would one wish it any other way. On every wall along the lengthy corridors there are photographs of those who

Трегубов Сергей

have taken part in the dance history of this city, from Elssler and Taglioni to Dudinskaya and Ulanova, and all the great teachers and choreographers besides. In the classrooms pictures of the famous composers, choreographers, and teachers look down on the current generation of students.

Grateful graduates frequently donate to the school gifts relating to ballet, as do visitors from abroad. One classroom boasts the presence of two large oil paintings by Mikhail Fokine that used to hang in his New York apartment on Riverside Drive. One of the portraits is of his wife, Vera, in the costume of a Russian boyar; the other is a self-portrait depicting the choreographer in a costume from *Jota Aragonesa.* Elsewhere throughout the building one is constantly reminded of the great names that have passed through Theatre Street—Kschessinskaya, Pavlova, Karsavina. In the scrapbooks they smile shyly in school groups, demurely dressed in their charming uniforms; on the walls they present another image, that of great ballerinas in the prime of their careers.

Most of the dancers who have recently experienced life in Theatre Street agree that it is not very different from the days Tamara Karsavina evoked so movingly in *Theatre Street.* The Tsar and Grand Dukes no longer arrive with their wives to have supper with the pretty graduating dancers; no longer are three-day holidays awarded as a favor by the Little Mother and Little Father, as the children called the Tsar and Tsarina. But the little girls still curtsy to visitors when they pass them in the long corridors, and the small boys politely bow their heads. It is a small but important indication of the respect that is shown to older people by these delightfully well mannered children. Sergiu suggested to me that it is this graciousness, learned from their first day at school, that makes the dancers so convincing in the Kirov's productions of the classics. When they mime aristocratic roles, they seem natural, because they have absorbed the tradition.

Good behavior, as well as the fostering of conscientious patterns of work, is an important part of the educational process at the Vaganova Institute. A notice board periodically lists the best students in three different categories: good behavior and all-around helpfulness to others, academic achievement, and a high standard in ballet. The student who has scored best in the three categories gets a special award. This is considered a very high honor.

The school day begins early. The children at the dormitory rise at seven A.M. They make their own beds, tidy up, and have breakfast before eight-thirty, when their first lessons begin. The full, complicated timetable for over five hundred students necessitates the posting of a schedule on the notice board, where children in all grades can check up at any time to see where they should be. With academic lessons and dance classes alternating in merry profusion throughout three floors of the school building, and studios and academic classrooms laid out on the many different levels of the school, often side by side, there is always plenty of rushing about as students strive to get to their next assignment on time, whether it be a piano lesson, gymnastics, or fencing. The corridors teem with the sounds of the school's varied activities.

"Please just listen; don't scribble, or you'll miss something."

Fortunately for both students and teachers, the canteen remains open throughout the day, and is always filled with students of all sizes. Early on they learn that they can never be sure when they will be free to eat their next meal. Artists with complicated schedules are used to this flexible life-style, and the children learn that this is how their lives will be if they succeed in becoming professional dancers.

Бабаков Ата.

Holding on to the barre, the students, boys and girls alike,
perform an assortment of pliés, battements tendus,
and ronds de jambes,
as well as fondus and frappés and much else besides,
all essential to the building of the right muscles for this
most demanding discipline.

The Vaganova Institute's curriculum of ballet lessons and stagecraft is astonishingly thorough and a source of envy to Westerners. In addition to the eight-year course in classical ballet, the students learn character dances such as the mazurka and czardas, their own Russian national dances, and historical dances like the gavotte, polonaise, polka, and minuet. Pas de deux classes and variation classes are regularly given, as well as classes in ballet mime and acting.

The boys also receive coaching in the art of fencing, which is
essential for such ballets as *Romeo and Juliet*, where the dancers
must simulate swordplay between Montagues and Capulets
in the streets and squares of Verona. An intensive
course in stage makeup is also included in the curriculum.

Alexander Minz, the contemporary of Rudolf Nureyev and Yuri Soloviev, and now a principal dancer with American Ballet Theatre, specializing in mime roles, recalls with delight the classes in theatrical improvisation. He himself had three years of drama school before entering the Vaganova Institute at the age of ten. A performance he saw of *Cinderella* with Dudinskaya and Sergeyev in the leading roles caused him to change the course of his life from acting to dance.

Chinko Rafique, formerly with the Royal Ballet and one-time principal dancer with the Zurich Ballet and the National Ballet of Iran, also was deeply impressed by the thoroughness of the acting classes. "In these classes we learned the dramatic roles, heroic parts like Spartacus. For instance, we learned all the intricacies of the love pas de deux in *Spartacus*, as well as many other ballets of a dramatic nature. We had one teacher who was a fantastic dramatic actress, Tatiana Smirova. She was extraordinary to work with and it was she who was given the task of bringing out the dramatic qualities of the pupils. All this was in the curriculum of the students in order that they should be released artistically, dramatically, and emotionally. It was a very specific part of our education to learn this part of the repertoire. For instance, if it was thought that a boy was talented classically but weak and uncertain in expression, he would be sent to Smirova. 'He's so timid. He can't express anything,' they would say. His glissade jeté is beautiful, but nothing comes out. We'll send him to Smirova.' That's how they used to work, you see. If they thought someone had talent, they would draw it out of him."

Early on in their training the children take part in performances at the Kirov Theatre. Just as in the nineteenth century, the smallest pupils find themselves sharing the stage with some of the most distinguished artists of the Soviet musical theatre. It's a wonderful training ground for these novice dancers, for they learn at firsthand how hard a dancer's life can be, as well as how glamorous and exciting. Backstage there are makeup specialists to assist the children, and other helpers to fix their hair and put on their costumes. By the time a girl is fifteen or sixteen she will be experienced enough to put on her own false eyelashes and pin up her long hair. But while the children are young, nothing is left to chance. In the wings there will always be a wardrobe assistant ready to help with needle and thread should an emergency arise, or simply to offer an encouraging word to the nervous.

Some of these small children retain the memories of their early stage experiences all their lives. Lubov Tchernicheva, for instance, recalls the occasion when she walked on as a child in the

opera *Faust*. The great singer Feodor Chaliapin was the
Mephistopheles, and Tchernicheva remembers him as "a towering
streak of crimson." Perhaps it is this proximity to the senior artists
of the Kirov Theatre that teaches the children how much effort
goes into the making of an artist. Galina Ulanova has written, "I
was still very young when I realized that airiness, beauty and
inspiration in the dance can be achieved only through the greatest
effort."

All the performances, whether in ballet or opera, require long
hours of rehearsals, costume fittings, and just plain hanging
around. After a day crammed with lessons and dance classes, it
can be exhausting. At times like these the comments of Alex
Tomoushin, a bright and mischievous thirteen-year-old, reverberate
with truth. During an outing with the school filmed for *The
Children of Theatre Street* the youngster looked at the camera and
candidly gave his views on what it is like to be a ballet student.
"Life is hard. Both my mother and my father are from families of
workers. A lot of the time things are hard at the school. Sometimes
I want to run away from it all. But when things go well, I accept it.
Of course my mother didn't want to let me go away to school,
because I'm her only child. And my father said, 'What kind of
work is dancing? When you get older you'll go to college—after
that you can dance.' I find the dance really hard work." Despite
this hard work, there is probably not a child at the school who
would be willing to change places with one outside.

U ntil the end of the 1960s the professional dancers of the Kirov
Ballet used to take class with such exceptional teachers as
Alexander Pushkin and Natalia Dudinskaya at the studios on Rossi
Street. Now the company dancers attend class and rehearse in
premises near the Kirov Theatre itself. Like the stage at the
theatre, all of the studios at Rossi Street are raked to precisely the
same proportions, which accustoms the children to performing on
the same sloping dimensions.

Sergiu Stefanschi remembers the thrill it gave him as a child
to see dancers who had delighted audiences in the theatre the
night before coming to the school to take class. "They used to be
so warm and friendly to us," he told me. "They would give us
photographs and signed point shoes, and were never too busy to
stop and have a few friendly words with us." Some of the leading
dancers are entrusted with teaching assignments, and it is not
uncommon to see a ballerina who has performed a leading role the
night before arrive at Theatre Street early the next day to pass on
her knowledge to a new generation.

The move of the company to its own premises adjoining the Kirov Theatre has had one disadvantage. It prevents the students at the school from viewing their favorites in class. Though it was officially discouraged, it became a custom for the children to peep around the doors of the studios to catch a glimpse of the great ones at work. The kindly teachers would turn a blind eye to the small enthusiastic faces, for they realized that this was something they had once done themselves. Nowadays the students have as their models the senior students who are about to graduate. The smaller children all pick out their favorites.

It is a common trait of the ballet child to be observant, and the Kirov children are no exception. Sergiu remembers the fun the children in his dormitory had imitating the technical moves they had seen on stage that night. Returning to the dormitory by special transport after the performance, they would try out the dancing they had seen their elders do. There would be much giggling, laughter, and horseplay, followed by a cold snack, served the younger children by the seniors. Lights had to be out by midnight. Robert Dornhelm remembers seeing other endings to these long days, when the children would return from a performance and fall straight into bed from sheer exhaustion.

At the strictly segregated dormitories one of the tasks of the matron in charge is to see that there is no fraternizing between the sexes and that rules are kept. In Tamara Geva's day, "We were made to speak softly, address our elders with respect, curtsy and speak to the boys only when it was absolutely necessary." As with children everywhere, however, natural high spirits sometimes erupt and have to be curbed, albeit gently. Rules exist, but as in educational institutions all over the world, most are for the comfort and convenience of the school as a whole.

If they have any free hours in the evening, between homework, rehearsals, and performances, the children are often found in the large recreation room where there is a television set. Here they can also read, write letters home, or indulge in some other quiet pursuit. Sometimes as a treat dances will be held to the music of a piano or records. Normally, though, the children have very little spare time after they have completed their daily chores.

For all the children, large and small, life revolves around the theatre, the school, and performances. Chinko Rafique told me that for him, "little else existed" when he was a student. Each ballet night sixteen passes are handed out to students. In the morning those who want to go to a performance apply at the office of the school director. "If they were feeling in a good mood they would say yes, but it used to be a hell of a battle," Chinko said with feeling. Sergiu Stefanschi remembers that many of the students unsuccessful in obtaining a pass would slip into the theatre unofficially and find themselves seats on the steps of the upper gallery. Others more fortunate found a nearer view of the stage.

In addition to free entrance to many performances, the children of the Vaganova Institute receive other privileges, among them brief vacations at the school's official country residences. For ten days in December the children are allowed a holiday in the countryside north of Leningrad, near the Finnish border. Here in the crisp air they sled, ski, and enjoy the winter's special joys. Natalia Makarova remembers these holidays with nostalgia. "It was such a fantastic time. As well as the winter sports, we went to movies and sometimes we used to have dances—dancing in my time was the foxtrot!—it was a place where romances started." In the spring there is another vacation, and in the months of July and August the school's residence on the Black Sea becomes a summer home for those who are unable to return to their families.

Talking to dancers who have passed through the Vaganova Institute, one cannot help being impressed by the breadth of their knowledge of outside life and culture. Far more than their Western colleagues, they are interested in the latest art exhibitions, books, and movies. "While young we learned that these things are important to us as artists," one graduate told me.

Another unifying experience shared by the Kirov dancers is that of having lived in Leningrad. In all of them, it seems, the city has left an indelible memory, and the dancers, as well as anyone who has known Leningrad, find themselves enriched by this monumentally lovely city, its museums, palaces, and its inhabitants. It is impossible to forget the bravery of the people of Leningrad during World War II, when for nine hundred days between 1941 and 1943 they endured the terrible blockade, under which nearly a quarter of the city's population died of starvation.

During this period the Kirov Ballet and the Vaganova Institute were evacuated to the city of Molotov (now Perm). Here a new school and company were later founded, carrying on the traditions the Kirov teachers left behind. Today Perm has one of the best companies and schools in the Soviet Union. Among its graduates are Nadzheda Pavlova, a young ballerina at the Bolshoi Ballet, and Galina Panov.

Several Leningrad dancers remained behind during the siege, among them Tatiana Vecheslova and Olga Jordan. They took part in volunteer work with the rest of the city's population, and there were times when they became so weak from hunger they could scarcely walk. Nevertheless, when the situation improved, these indomitable individuals improvised concerts and performances in camps and hospitals. Theatre Street fortunately emerged from the horrors of the war comparatively unscathed. Although the Germans bombarded Leningrad mercilessly from the air and much of the city was demolished, only one shell hit the school building. Surrounded on all sides by explosions, the foundations of the two-hundred-year-old building miraculously remained firm.

During the war the teachers at the school, missing their pupils, appealed to the civic authorities for permission to recruit local children from schools and Pioneer Palaces. Permission was given and one hundred applications were received after an enrollment notice was posted outside the school. Twenty children were eventually chosen. They had tragic stories to tell. Nearly all had lost one or both parents in the war, either through starvation or in action at the front. The city rallied to help the school with its needs. Extra rations were provided and clothes donated for the needy pupils. Olga Jordan, one of the most heroic of those who endured those terrible times, and who did so much toward building the morale of those remaining in Leningrad, was awarded a medal of honor for her part in the city's defense.

It is perhaps the shared experience of having survived so much together that has made the older teachers so loyal to the school, its traditions, and the children in its charge. Olga Jordan, Rotislav Zakharov's first Zarema in *The Fountains of Bakhchisarai,* and a contemporary of Ulanova, died just recently, but during her life she was regarded as one of the school's most outstanding teachers. One of her pupils was a brilliantly talented young dancer, Ludmilla Svetlieva. Sadly for the Kirov Ballet, Svetlieva went into films and never returned to ballet. In true Hollywood style she was "discovered" by eagle-eyed talent scouts who were searching for the right young girl to portray Natasha in *War and Peace.*

Another teacher of the old school who for years was director of the school was Nikolai Ivanovsky. Sasha Minz remembers this one-time colleague of Balanchine's as a man of extraordinary culture and elegance who taught the children good manners by his example. "His presence was very beneficial to the school," Sasha told me, "because he respected deeply the traditions of the past." There are still teachers, such as the legendary Dudinskaya, who recall the traditions of the Imperial Ballet, but today many teachers come from outside. Oleg Briansky, artistic director for the film *The*

Children of Theatre Street, told me of a conversation he had with one of the current teachers at the school who regrets the passing of the old generation. The new teachers, she feels, do not have the same strong background. Nevertheless, it is felt that Vaganova's teaching methods must be open to fresh influences, and that no syllabus can remain unchanged, but must adapt to changing circumstances, different dancers and audiences.

At the Vaganova Choreographic Institute there is something called the "method cabinet." This is not a piece of furniture but rather a regular gathering at which the staff discusses theories of teaching and methods of execution. Interesting new ideas and innovations are explored and worked out in practice. If found to be beneficial, they may be absorbed into the syllabus of the school. This open attitude, which maintains that the teaching of ballet is always in a state of development, is almost certainly what Vaganova would have wished.

One thing that never changes is the early encouragement the
children receive to explore the feel of the stage. At yearly
examinations in the school theatre before the entire staff, in an
atmosphere something like a performance, the pupils' progress is
checked and constructive suggestions are made. On these
occasions it is not just the child who is on display but also the
teacher.

In addition, concert galas are given on special occasions throughout the year. These are performed before an invited audience of relatives, friends, faculty, and certain pupils. The little theatre, which seats between one hundred fifty and two hundred people, is part of the school complex, and its tiny stage has seen the first performances of many great dancers from Imperial days onward. The galas often form part of the celebration for such special days in the Soviet calendar as the Seventh of November and the First of May, and, according to Natalia Makarova, they provide some nervous times. It is at these special events that word gets around of the talent that is being nurtured at the school.

Makarova, who was a pupil of Elena Sherepina, was regarded
as extremely promising from the very beginning. A late starter, she
was placed in the accelerated six-year course. The year before she
officially graduated, Makarova performed at the annual graduation
performance as the partner of Yuri Soloviev, whose graduation
year it was. Together they danced the Blue Bird pas de deux.
Soloviev was later to become one of the greatest of the Kirov's
male dancers. A perfect stylist with exquisite feet, he was
physically not unlike Nijinsky, and like his famous predecessor, he
was noted for his soaring jumps and his ability to hover in the air.

When the Kirov Ballet first danced in London in 1961 Soloviev became an enormous favorite with the audience, so much so that when it was discovered that he was not scheduled to dance the Blue Bird on the final night of the company's season at the Royal Opera House, the regular gallery-goers organized a petition to the management urging a change in the casting. This unusual request was met, and Soloviev went on to receive a thunderous and prolonged ovation. When Soloviev committed suicide, in 1977, it was a tragedy not only for the company but also for the dancer's many friends.

When a boy or girl reaches the age of fifteen or sixteen, he or she begins to learn the Kirov's repertoire. The coaching the youngsters receive in these repertoire classes is done as carefully as if they were already professionals. Self-reliance is emphasized from an early age. If a young dancer is given a role to learn, it is because he is considered equipped to handle it. Thus, by the time they graduate, many of the older pupils have absorbed a fair amount of the Kirov repertory. For the actual graduation performance the teacher works out with the pupil what role he or she is best suited to. Naturally the year's most talented dancers are given the most prominent roles in which to display themselves.

For months before graduation at the end of June, pupils and teachers work with maximum intensity to prepare thoroughly for the big day. This is the last occasion for many of the students to appear on the Kirov stage, for there are normally less than ten vacancies in the Kirov company in any one year.

Considerable tension and excitement build up as the examinations and the graduation performance draw near. Those taking part think and talk about little else.

*"It's a very emotional time for everyone,
when all of us find out our future, our destiny."*

Chinko Rafique remembers that the students "went at it step by step, the entire thing, about three times a week. The teachers were total perfectionists, and nothing escaped them, not the minutest thing. They were determined that we should give our very best. Naturally it was important to them as well as to us that we look like true professionals."

The dance examinations given prior to graduation are attended by school authorities and representatives from companies all over the Soviet Union. The fate of each graduate hangs mainly on the results of this exposure. The dancers' careers are not in their own hands but totally in the hands of the hierarchy. Makarova says of this period, "It's a very emotional time for everyone, when all of us find out our future, our destiny. There are a lot of tears from some who expect that they will go to one place, one city, and instead they are sent to another."

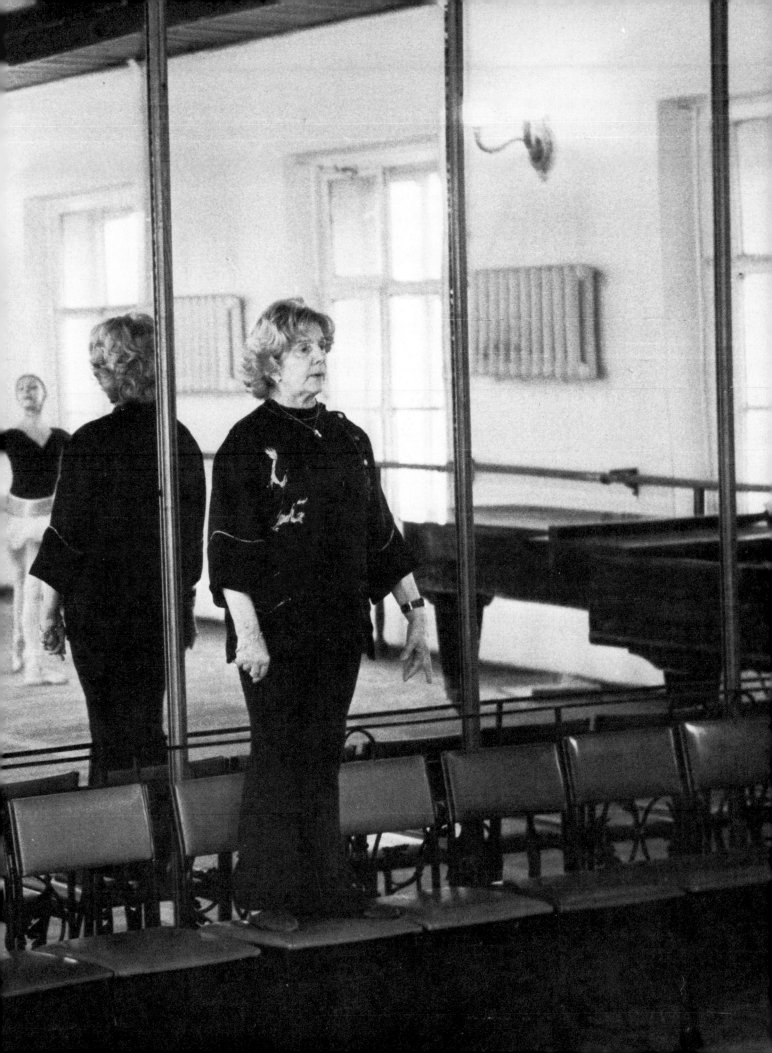

By the time of the graduation performance the dancers have been rehearsed to the very edges of their nerves. They are treated as professionals by their teachers, not for the first time in their lives but never more seriously, for on this occasion they must do justice to the great traditions of the theatre in which they will perform.

The day arrives, and the costumes are fitted. Makeup and hair are carefully arranged. The audience pours into the 1790-seat gold and blue theatre—family, friends, and the most knowledgeable of Leningrad's balletomanes. The buzz of talk hushes as the conductor takes his place. Backstage the dancers hear the applause. They struggle to keep their nerves under control.

Each dancer knows the role he or she must perform. It only remains for them to do their best. Some will dance as never before. Others will be bitterly disappointed in themselves. All dancers are hard on themselves, and are rarely satisfied even when others consider them perfect.

When the curtain is brought down, there are congratulations, flowers, embraces, and tears. Friends, relatives, and dancers crowd around the graduating students. There are more curtain calls, more embraces. Excitement is heavy, but there is a sadness too, for it is a time of parting, and many of the graduates will be dispersed far and wide throughout the Soviet Union. Foreign students return to their own countries. Some will go to one of the thirty or more companies scattered throughout the huge country of Russia, such as those in Novosibirsk or Sverdlovsk. Others may find themselves remaining in Leningrad, if not at the Kirov then perhaps with Leningrad's second company, the Maly, or with the Choreographic Miniatures, also located in the city. This small and by Russian standards avant-garde company specializes in the new and different. Until his recent death, it was run by the much loved and unusually innovative choreographer Leonid Jacobson, but now the company is directed by Askold Makarov, once known for his powerful characterization of Spartacus with the Kirov Ballet.

Certain dancers with a flair for character work are approached to join folk-dance companies such as the Moiseyev. These companies, like the Bolshoi and the Kirov, tour all over the world, and audiences respond to their vitality and warmth. Soviet authorities know that these tours are an effective way to win goodwill for their country. But wherever their careers take them, all who graduate from the Vaganova Choreographic Institute retain memories of their years at Theatre Street.

When I asked Chinko Rafique what it was that he loved best about his years at the world's most famous dance academy, he thought for a moment and replied, "The fact that *they* loved it—all those wonderful artists. That they were committed, absolutely, body, mind, and soul, to dance. That was really the essence, the greatness, of the Kirov Theatre, and of the school. It was the conviction they possessed. Simply: 'I am an artist. I am. I am a dancer.' "

Acknowledgments

I am particularly grateful to the group of artists who turned my idea into reality. For their generous contributions I would like to thank: Princess Grace of Monaco, a dedicated and loyal supporter of the film; Robert Dornhelm, a talented director who was extremely helpful in every area; Oleg Briansky, whose in-depth knowledge of dance artistry and contacts at the school made everything easier; Jean Dalrymple, whose wisdom and experience never failed us; Ted Landreth, a trusted friend who was always available; Karl Kofler, surely a life saver; Tina Frese, a brilliant film editor; Mireille Briane and Linda Dagenais, whose artistic abilities deserve a special tribute; the employees of the Novosti Press Agency, whose allegiances to the film's successful completion were unremitting; Patricia Barnes, without whom this book could not be what it is; Olga Zaferatos and Viking Penguin Inc., who believed in the importance of the film and the merits of the school.

E.M.

I would first of all like to thank Earle Mack, Robert Dornhelm, and Oleg Briansky for sharing with me their observations and experiences during the filming of *The Children of Theatre Street*. They were helpful and encouraging at all times. Beth Gutcheon's film script, so evocative and descriptive, was also a welcome source of inspiration.

In addition I am deeply grateful to all those I interviewed: choreographers, teachers, and dancers, who are all fortunate enough to have spent part of their life in Leningrad at the Vaganova School. Tamara Geva, Yuri Grigorovich, Nora Kovach, Natalia Makarova, Hans Meister, Alexander Minz, Rudolf Nureyev, Valery Panov, Chinko Rafique, Sergiu Stefanschi, and Gabriella Taub-Darvish have all contributed so much to dance, and I was touched and happy that they found time to talk to me about their memories.

Genna Smakov and Suzanne Massie read through my final text. Their experienced eyes saved me, I hope, from making too many errors of fact and their suggestions were always apt and constructive. To both of them my sincere appreciation. My sister, Rosemary Winckley, typed the final manuscript, bouyed me at every turn, and also lent photographs from her precious collection for use in this book. Finally my husband, Clive, must be thanked for his advice, patience, and interest throughout the preparation of this book.

P.B.

Photo Credits

Mireille Briane: pages 78–79; *Robert Dornhelm/Karl Kofler:* pages 48, 51, 53, 54–55, 56–57, 60 bottom, 61 top, 68, 71, 76, 82, 83, 84–85, 88, 89, 96, 100, 101, 102, 103, 106, 107, 109, 111, 120–121, 126, 127, 128, 138, 141 ; *Alexander Ougladnikov:* pages 46 – 47 top , 60 top, 61 bottom, 62, 63, 64, 65, 66, 67, 69, 74, 75, 80–81, 86, 87, 90–91, 94–95, 99, 104, 105, 112, 113, 114, 115, 116, 117, 118, 119, 122, 123, 124, 125, 129, 130, 131, 133, 134–135, 136–137; *Rosemary Winckley Collection:* pages 12, 33, 34, 36, 37, 38, 40, 42 , 41. The drawings reproduced on pages 58, 59, 72, 73, 77, and 93 were made by the children.

Bibliography

Books

Barnes, Clive. "Fifty Years of Soviet Ballet." *The Soviet Union: The Fifty Years.* Edited by Harrison E. Salisbury. New York: The New York Times and Harcourt, Brace & World, Inc., 1967.

Beaumont, Cyril, compiler and translator. *A Miscellany for Dancers.* London: published by Cyril Beaumont, 1934.

Beresovsky, V. Bogdanov. *Ulanova and the Development of the Soviet Ballet.* Translated by Stephen Garry and Joan Lawson. London: MacGibbon & Kee, 1952.

Buckle, Richard. *Nijinsky.* New York: Simon & Schuster, 1971.

Cecchetti, Enrico. *Master of the Russian Ballet: Memoirs of Enrico Cecchetti.* London: Hutchinson & Co., 1922.

Clarke, Mary, and Crisp, Clement. *Ballet: An Illustrated History.* New York: Universe Books, 1973.

Demidov, Alexander. *The Russian Ballet Past & Present.* Moscow: Novosti Press, and New York: Doubleday & Company, 1977.

Duncan, Isadora. *My Life.* London: Victor Gollancz Ltd., 1928.

Flitch, J. E. Crawford. *Modern Dancing and Dancers.* London: Grant Richards Ltd., 1912.

Fokine, Michel. *Fokine, Memoirs of a Ballet Master.* Anatole, Chujoy, ed. Translated by Vitale Fokine. Boston: Little, Brown & Company, 1961.

Geva, Tamara. *Split Seconds, A Remembrance.* New York and London: Harper & Row, 1972.

Haskell, Arnold. *A Picture History of Ballet.* London: Hulton Press, 1954.

Haskell, Arnold. *The Russian Genius in Ballet.* Oxford: Pergamon Press, 1963.

Karsavina, Tamara. *Theatre Street.* New York: E. P. Dutton, Inc., 1930.

Kirov Ballet Souvenir 1961. New York: Sol Hurok, 1961.

Kschessinska (Kschessinskaya), Matilda. *Dancing in Petersburg.* Translated by Arnold Haskell. London: Victor Gollancz, 1960.

Legat, Nicolas. *Ballet Russe: Memoirs of Nicolas Legat.* London: Methuen & Co. Ltd., 1939.

Lifar, Serge. *A History of the Russian Ballet.* Translated by Arnold Haskell. London: Hutchinson, 1954.

Lynham, Deryck. *The Chevalier Noverre, Father of Modern Ballet.* London: Sylvan Press, 1950.

Onassis, Jacqueline, ed. *In the Russian Style.* New York: The Viking Press, 1976.

Percival, John. *Nureyev: A Biography.* New York: C. P. Putnam Sons, 1975.

Petipa, Marius. *Russian Ballet Master, the Memoirs of Marius Petipa.* Lillian Moore, ed. New York: A. & C. Black, 1958.

Nureyev, Rudolf. *Nureyev: An Autobiography.* Introduced by Alexander Bland. London: Hodder & Stoughton, 1962.

Roslavleva, Natalia. *Era of the Russian Ballet.* New York: E. P. Dutton & Co. Inc., 1966.

Samachson, Dorothy and Joseph. *The Russian Ballet and Three of Its Masterpieces.* New York: Lothrop, Lee & Shepard Company, 1971.

Slonimsky, Yuri, and others. *Soviet Ballet.* New York: Philosophical Library, 1947.

Svetloff, Valerian. *Anna Pavlova.* London: The British-Continental Press Ltd., 1930.

Swift, Mary Grace. *The Art of the Dance in the U.S.S.R.* Notre Dame, Indiana: University of Notre Dame Press, 1968.

Swift, Mary Grace. *A Loftier Flight.* New York: Wesleyan Press, and London: Pitman Publishing, 1974.

Taper, Bernard. *Balanchine.* New York: Harper & Row, 1963.

Winter, Marian Hannah. *The Pre-Romantic Ballet.* New York: Dance Horizons, 1974.

Periodicals

Ballet, London (published in the 1940s and 1950s).

The Ballet. (Russian Ballet League periodical) London, December 1946.

The Ballet Annual, London (published yearly from 1947–1964).

Dance and Dancers, London.

Dance Magazine, New York.

Dance News, New York.

The Dancing Times, London.

Daniel, David. "Conversation with Alexander Minz." *Christopher Street,* August 1976.

Newsweek, May 19, 1975. Baryshnikov cover story by Hubert Saal.

Slonimsky, Yuri. "Balanchine, the Early Years." *Ballet Review,* New York, 1977/78, Volume 6, No. 3.

Time, May 19, 1975. Baryshnikov cover story.

Index

Acis et Galatea, 37
Alexander I, Tsar, 15, 17, 22
Alexis, Tsar, 13
Andreyanova, Elena, 27, 29
Angiolini, Gasparo, 15, 16, 17
Anna, Empress, 13, 14
Apres-midi d'un Faune, L', 38
Armeiskaya, Angelina, 8, 46, 58, 66, 68
Ashton, Sir Frederick, 39
Away with Sadness, 33

Bakst, Léon, 39
Balabina, Fea, 42
Balanchine, George, 6, 9, 39, 40, 49, 98
Baryshnikov, Mikhail, 9, 12, 45
Bayadère, La, 30
Beaumont, Cyril, 27
Benois, Alexander, 39
Biron, Johan, 13
Blasis, Carlo, 34
Bolm, Adolfe, 39
Boublikov, Timofei Seminovich, 15
Bournonville, August, 28, 32
Briansky, Oleg, 6, 7, 9, 98-99
Brianza, Carlotta, 33-34

Cacucha, La, 28
Canziani, Joseph, 17
Caracole, 6
Carnaval, 37, 38
Catherine the Great, 15, 16
Cavos, Alberto, 28
Cecchetti, Enrico, 33, 34, 41
Cerna, Michaela, 47
Cerrito, Fanny, 27
Cervantes, Miguel de, 30
Chabukiani, Vakhtang, 12, 41
Chaliapin, Feodor, 39, 93
Chevalier-Bressolles, Mme., 18
Chevalier-Bressolles, Peicam de, 18
Chopiniana, 37
Chujoy, Anatole, 42
Cinderella, 34, 92
Coppélia, 29
Corsaire, Le, 45

Dalrymple, Jean, 7, 8
Danilova, Alexandra, 39
Danilova, Maria, 20-21, 72
Daphnis and Chloë, 37
Dauberval, Jean, 19, 28
Daughter of Pharaoh, 29
Denby, Edwin, 6
Diaghilev, Sergei, 38, 39-40, 41
Diana and Acteon, 44
Didelot, Charles Louis, 18-20, 21, 22, 23, 24-25, 27, 28, 29, 34
Don Quixote, 30, 37, 43
Dornhelm, Robert, 6, 7, 8, 66, 96
Drigo, Riccardo, 31
Dudinskaya, Natalia, 12, 42, 44, 46, 73, 92, 93, 98
Duncan, Isadora, 37-38
Duport, Louis, 21, 24

Elizabeth, Empress, 15
Elssler, Fanny, 27, 28, 29, 41, 73
Esmeralda, 28, 43

Federova, Nadezhda, 46
Fedicheva, Kaleria, 45
Fessetchko, Antonia, 59
Fille Mal Gardée, La, 28, 37
Flames of Paris, The, 43
Fokine, Mikhail, 34, 36, 37-38, 39, 40, 43, 73
Fokine, Vera, 73
Fountains of Bakhchisarai, The 43, 98
Frangopolo, Marietta, 72
Frese, Tina, 8
Fusano, Antonio, 14

Gagarin, Prince, 24, 25
Gautier, Théophile, 28, 30
Gayane, 45
Gedeonov, Alexander, 25, 27
Gerdt, Elizaveta, 40, 41, 42
Gerdt, Pavel, 30, 33, 34, 38, 40, 41
Geva, Tamara, 39, 49, 58, 96
Giselle, 27, 28, 43, 45
Glazunov, Alexander, 31
Glinka, Mikhail, 24
Glushkovsky, Adam, 20, 21-22, 25

Goethe, Johann Wolfgang von, 18
Goleizovsky, Kasyan, 40
Gorshakova, Maria, 37
Gorsky, Alexander, 38
Grace, Princess, 9
Grahn, Lucille, 27
Gridin, Anatole, 43
Grigorovich, Yuri, 42, 43, 49
Grisi, Carlotta, 27
Gusev, Piotr, 41
Gutcheon, Beth, 9

Harlequinade, 31
Haskell, Arnold, 35
Hilferding van Weven, Frantz, 15
Holtz, Nikolai, 24
Hunchback of Notre-Dame, The, 45

Ikonina, Maria, 20
Istomina, Avdotia, 23, 72
Ivanov, Lev, 31-32, 41
Ivanovsky, Nikolai, 98

Jacobson, Leonid, 43, 139
Jeux, 38
Johansson, Christian, 37, 30, 32-33, 34
Jordan, Olga, 42, 97-98
Jota Aragonesa, 73

Kafka, Lubomir, 47
Karsavin, Platon, 38
Karsavina, Tamara, 12, 33, 35, 37, 38, 39, 73
Katerina, the Serf Ballerina, 43
King Candaules, 40
Kingdom of the Shades, The, 31
Kofler, Karl, 7
Kolosova, Evgenia, 21, 24
Kolpakova, Irina, 42, 43
Kovach, Nora, 41-42
Kschessinskaya, Matilda, 33, 34, 35, 36, 73
Kutaisov, Count, 18

Landé, Jean Baptiste, 13-14
Landreth, Ted, 8
Laurencia, 43, 45

Lavronsky, Leonid, 43
Legat, Nikolai, 32, 34, 36, 41, 58
Legat, Sergei, 33, 36, 37
Legend of Love, The, 44
Legnani, Pierina, 33-34
Lenin, Nikolai, 49
Le Picq, Charles, 12, 17, 19
Lepri, Giovanni, 34-35
Limido, Giovanna, 33
Little Hump-backed Horse, The,
   28-29, 43
Locatelli, Giovanni, 14
Longus, 37
Lopukhov, André, 43
Lopukhov, Feodor, 40, 43
Louis XIV, King, 58
Lucom, Yelena, 36-37, 41
Lunacharsky, Anatole, 40

Magic Mirror, The, 35
Makarov, Askold, 139
Makarova, Natalia, 9, 12, 43, 44, 45,
   58, 97, 104-106, 118
Maria Theresa, Empress, 15
Marie, Empress, 35
Massine, Léonide, 39
Maximova, Ekaterina, 42
Mazilier, Joseph, 29
Minkus, Ludwig, 31
Minz, Alexander, 44, 45, 92, 98
Mordkin, Mikhail, 39
Mouravieva, Marfa, 28, 29

Naryshkin, Alexander, 18
Nicholas I, Tsar, 26
Nicholas II, Tsar, 34
Nijinska, Bronislava, 39
Nijinsky, Vaslav, 12, 37, 38-39, 45, 58
Nikitina, Varvara, 34
Noverre, Jean Georges, 15, 16, 17, 19
Novitskaya, Anastasia, 20, 25
Nureyev, Rudolf, 9, 12, 43, 44, 92
Nutcracker, The, 32, 37, 45

Obukhov, Mikhail, 38
Ossipenko, Alla, 42, 43, 44
Oumpikhin, Yuri, 46

Panov, Galina, 45, 97
Panov, Valery, 12, 42-43, 45
Paquita, 29
Paul, Tsar, 18
Pavlova, Anna, 12, 33, 35, 36, 37, 38,
   39, 73
Pavlova, Nadezhda, 97

Perrot, Jules, 27-28, 29
Peter the Great, 12, 13, 14, 49
Petipa, Jean, 29
Petipa, Marie, 30, 34
Petipa, Marius, 27, 29-32, 33, 34, 35,
   40
Petit, Roland, 45
Petrushka, 37, 38
Pisarev, Alexei, 43
Plisetskaya, Maya, 42
Poirot, Auguste, 18, 19
Ponamarov, Vladimir, 43
Preobrajenskaya, Olga, 36
Prince Igor, 37
Prisoner of the Caucasus, The, 23, 24
Prokofiev, Sergei, 43
Psyche et l'Amour, 21
Pugni, Cesare, 28, 31
Pushkin, Alexander (poet), 23, 32
Pushkin, Alexander (teacher), 43, 44,
   45, 93

Rafique, Chinko, 92, 96, 110, 139
Raymonda, 31, 43
Red Poppy, The, 43
Romeo and Juliet, 43, 88
Rosati, Carolina, 29
Roslavleva, Natalia, 36
Rossi, Carlo, 12, 13, 26
Rossi, Gertrude, 12
Ruses d'Amour, 31

Sacre du Printemps, Le, 39
Saint-Léon, Arthur, 28-29, 30
Sarovschikova, Marie, 29
Satinella, 29
Schéhérazade, 37
Semenov, Vladilen, 43
Semenyaka, Ludmillia, 49
Semeonova, Marina, 12, 35, 41, 42, 58
Sergeyev, Konstantin, 14, 41, 43, 46,
   92
Sergueeff, Nikolai, 37
Shakhovsky, Alexander A., 22
Shavrov, Boris, 43, 44
Shelest, Alla, 42
Sherepina, Elena, 106
Sizova, Alla, 43
Sleeping Beauty, The, 31, 32, 34, 36,
   37, 40-41, 43
Slonimsky, Yuri, 15, 23
Smirnova, Tatiana, 27, 29
Smirova, Tatiana, 92
Soloviev, Yuri, 43, 45, 92, 106-107
Soymonov, Major General, 16-17

Spartacus, 92
Spectre de la Rose, Le, 37, 38
Spessivtzeva, Olga, 39, 40-41
Stanislavsky, Konstantin, 44
Stefanschi, Sergiu, 72, 73, 93, 96-97
Stone Flower, The, 43-44
Struchkova, Raissa, 42
Svetlieva, Ludmilla, 98
Svetlov, Valerian, 36
Swan Lake, 31, 32, 34, 43, 45, 58
Swift, Mary Grace, 24
Sylphide, La, 26
Sylphides, Les, 37, 38

Taglioni, Filippo, 26
Taglioni, Marie, 21, 24, 26, 27, 28, 41,
   73
Taub-Darvash, Gabriella, 42
Tchaikovsky, Piotr Ilich, 31
Tchernicheva, Lubov, 92-93
Teliakovsky, Colonel Vladimir, 35, 37
Timoushin, Alec, 8, 46, 93
Titus, Antoine Dauchy, 29
Trefilova, Vera, 36
Tyl Eulenspiegel, 38

Ulanova, Galina, 12, 35, 41, 42, 43, 73,
   93, 98

Vaganova, Agrippina, 35, 41-43, 49,
   58, 99
Vainonen, Vassily, 43
Valberkh, Ivan, 17-18, 19, 21
Vandoyer, J. L., 36
Vazem, Ekaterina, 31, 41
Vecheslova, Tatiana, 97-98
Vestris, Gaetan, 19, 28, 32
Vikulov, Sergei, 43
Vinogradov, Oleg, 45
Volkova, Vera, 42
Voltaire, 17
Voronzova, Lena, 8, 47, 68
Vsevolojski, Ivan S., 31, 33, 35

Werther, 18
Wolkonsky, Prince Sergei, 35

Yelagin, Ivan P., 16
Yusupov, Prince, 17, 18

Zakharov, Rotislav, 43, 98
Zubkovskaya, Inna, 43-44
Zucchi, Virginia, 33, 34